Scripture Discussion Commentary 3

SCRIPTURE DISCUSSION COMMENTARY 3

*Series editor:* Laurence Bright

# Histories I

| | |
|--:|:--|
| **Judges** | *Hamish Swanston* |
| **1 and 2 Samuel** | *Hamish Swanston* |
| **1 and 2 Kings** | *Hamish Swanston* |
| **Ruth** | *Laurence Bright* |

**ACTA Foundation**
Adult Catechetical Teaching Aids
Chicago, Illinois

First published 1971
ACTA Foundation (Adult Catechetical Teaching Aids),
4848 N. Clark Street, Chicago, Illinois 60640

Nihil obstat : John M. T. Barton STD LSS *Censor*
Imprimatur : + Victor Guazzelli *Vicar General*
Westminster, 30 June 1971

2540

Library of Congress number 71–173033
ISBN 0 87946 002 4
Made and printed in Great Britain by
William Clowes & Sons, Limited
London, Beccles and Colchester

# Contents

**Ruth**   *Laurence Bright*                                    167

# General Introduction

A few of the individual units which make up this series of biblical commentaries have already proved their worth issued as separate booklets. Together with many others they are now grouped together in a set of twelve volumes covering almost all the books of the old and new testaments—a few have been omitted as unsuitable to the general purpose of the series.

That purpose is primarily to promote discussion. This is how these commentaries differ from the others that exist. They do not cover all that could be said about the biblical text, but concentrate on the features most likely to get lively conversation going—those, for instance, with special relevance for later developments of thought, or for life in the church and world of today. For this reason passages of narrative are punctuated by sets of questions designed to get a group talking, though the text of scripture, helped by the remarks of the commentator, should have already done just that.

For the text is what matters. Individuals getting ready for a meeting, the group itself as it meets, should always have the bible centrally present, and use the commentary only as a tool. The bibliographies will help those wishing to dig deeper.

What kinds of group can work in this way? Absolutely

any. The bible has the reputation of being difficult, and in some respects it is, but practice quickly clears up a lot of initial obstacles. So parish groups of any kind can and should be working on it. The groups needn't necessarily already exist, it is enough to have a few like-minded friends and to care sufficiently about finding out what the bible means. Nor need they be very large; one family could be quite enough. High schools (particularly in the senior year), colleges and universities are also obvious places for groups to form. If possible they should everywhere be ecumenical in composition: though all the authors are Roman catholics, there is nothing sectarian in their approach.

In each volume there are two to four, or occasionally more, studies of related biblical books. Each one is self-contained; it is neither necessary nor desirable to start at the beginning and plough steadily through. Take up, each time, what most interests you—there is very little in scripture that is actually dull! Since the commentaries are by different authors, you will discover differences of outlook, in itself a matter for discussion. Above all, remember that getting the right general approach to reading the bible is more important than answering any particular question about the text—and that this approach only comes with practice.

LAURENCE BRIGHT

# Introduction to Judges, Samuel, Kings

*Hamish Swanston*

The five books of the bible which concern us for most of this volume, Judges, 1 and 2 Samuel, 1 and 2 Kings, belong together not primarily because they form a continuous narrative, for often they present a doubling-back upon material already covered, nor because they represent a set of traditions of a uniform age and historical value, for they are certainly collections of oddly disparate material, but because they are the product of one impressive group of Hebrew historians who hoped to show in their writing how the history of their people should be interpreted. In making sense of their history these writers impressed various kinds of older writing to their service, folk tale and spell, treasurer's accounts and priestly ritual books, soldier's stories and dervishes' dreams. All were brought into the service of one great idea.

That idea is of Israel coming to grief whenever the people went a-whoring after strange gods and, though repenting each time at the moment when the cause of their ruin was appreciated, never fully learning the lesson of obedience to the loving will of Yahweh. The historians took it as the criterion of faithfulness to the will of Yahweh that the people should be recognising their duty to worship in the central shrine of Jerusalem. History is seen through liturgical spectacles.

Since this idea dominates the shape of the book of Deuteronomy, it is commonly agreed that the editors of these histories came from a group of Hebrew writers who also composed that book, perhaps just before and perhaps just after the exile, and these editors are therefore called 'the deuteronomists'. Perhaps their view of history will be the more readily appreciated if some account is given here of the compilation of these histories.

## Judges

The material included in our present text has been transmitted through various re-tellings. A great deal of the material is evidently very old. The song of triumph in chapter 5 is almost certainly the oldest piece of historical writing in the old testament, and was sung perhaps at the camp feast immediately after the defeat of the Philistines. Other narratives or sections of narratives of the book are ancient remembrances of the tribal heroes and have all the vivacity of their primitive recitation.

Some of these early tales and poems were collected in bundles quite early in their lives. The *Book of Jasher* and the *Book of the Wars of Yahweh* have left their names behind, but most of these early collections disappeared from the moment that the deuteronomists finished their rummaging and placed their sources in the waste-paper basket.

Other sources, of a kind more likely to have been handed on by oral recitation, were probably extant for much longer, running in parallel with the written versions. Though oral tradition is not necessarily less exact in reproducing an earlier telling, as anyone who has had to tell a story more than once to a small child will attest, the camp-fire recitals may have been responsible for the conflating of tales originally distinct, like the narratives of Jabin and Sisera in chapter 4 of Judges, or those of Gideon and Jerubbaal in chapters 6–9, and the two tales of Micah in chapters 17 and 18.

It seems likely, though all such talk is of guesses, that in the ninth century BC, a period of renewed interest in history, a Jerusalem scribe set himself to make a coherent narrative from the written and oral traditions received from the period before the kings. His account of the history was probably not quite the same in form as our present text. He seems to have placed the tales of our chapters 17, 18 and 19 rather earlier than we now have them, for in their present position between the stories of Samson and Eli they interrupt the account of the people 'in the days of the Philistines'. And since the death of Samson is not a particularly good point to end a narrative of this patriotic kind, probably the scribal history included material that we now find in the first chapters of I Samuel. Certainly the grand summary of 1 Samuel 12:7–11 would have made a proper closing passage for the Judges material.

After this first scribal construction other writers in the eighth and seventh centuries tampered with the ninth-century work. And then at the beginning of the sixth century, or perhaps some decades on in that century, an editor who belonged to the deuteronomist group took the Judges material in hand. He spent some effort in making the material of Jgs 2:6–16:3 conform to his view of history. The Hebrews are there shewn to be ever running after false gods and never learning the necessity of obedience to Yahweh. This historian had probably taken a part in the earlier revision of the material included in our Kings and Samuel. Certainly the deuteronomic character of the general introduction, 2:6–3:6, and the particular prefaces to the individual tales in Judges is plain, and equally evident is it that the body of each of these stories, except that of Othniel, is free of the peculiar deuteronomist emphasis.

The deuteronomist Judges almost certainly did not include our chapters 17, 18, 19–21, for these do not have the deuteronomist introductions. These last sections of our present text seem to have been rescued from their abandonment by the deuteronomistic editor through a final editor who could not bear to lose them but did not know where they had originally been set in the history. He therefore tacked them on to the end of the account the deuteronomist had left him. Perhaps this last editor himself added to the old material the body of chapter 20 and the first fourteen verses of chapter 21 which have a late vocabulary and seem to present the ecclesiastical attitudes of those who composed the books of Chronicles.

It is, however, the deuteronomist editor who has fixed for us the shape and tone of the book as we have it:

> Then the Israelites did what was evil in the sight of the Lord, by serving the Baals and forsaking the Lord, the God of their fathers, who had brought them out of the land of Egypt, and by running after alien gods, from among the gods of the peoples that surrounded them, and paying homage to them, so that they provoked the Lord to jealousy. Thus they forsook the Lord and served Baals and Ashtarts. Then the anger of the Lord blazed against Israel, so that he delivered them into the power of plunderers who plundered them, and he sold them into the power of their enemies around them so that they were no longer able to withstand their enemies [Jgs 2:11–15].

This deuteronomist thesis is to be seen also at Jgs 3:7 and 12, 4:1 and 6:1, passages which may be compared with

Deut 4:25, 9:18 and 17:2, 1 Sam 15:19, 2 Sam 12:9, 1 Kgs 15:26, and 2 Kgs 3:2 among many other such places.

The book is dominated by the deuteronomistic emphasis on the necessity of maintaining the pure cult of Yahweh in Israel. In the balance against the faithlessness of the people the editor placed the institution of the *shopet*—the judge. He is a man given to the people by Yahweh that he might lead them to a victory and a peace only attainable through an acknowledgement of Yahweh's divine order. And in the last section of the great history we are presented with a see-saw between periods of infidelity and periods of prosperity when the people, repenting of their sin, follow the advice of the judge.

Judges arrive on the Israelite scene by various processes, and not all these processes are immediately recognisable as divine sendings. Jephthah, Jgs 10:16—18, is said to be given by the Lord, but his election is the result of a debate among the leaders of Gilead, and later Eli is evidently recognised as judge among the people though there is no suggestion of how the divine call came to him or how he was accepted by the people.

The historian suggests that the judges were saviours and governors for the whole confederacy of tribes, but this description is simply part of his overall attempt to emphasise the national character of his history. He omits any element which might suggest the possibility of the tribes acting in separation, and he conceals the tribal character of the judges. These men were in fact merely the momentary leaders of particular tribes and had little importance for any but their own tribal settlement. Nor is the historian to be believed when he makes the judges he knows about follow one another in chronological sequence. Their work certainly over-lapped at some periods.

The historian has made of a set of odd incidents a continuous history, and of local heroes a national saga, and he has done this through the construction of an artificial time sequence, cf, eg, Jgs 3:7–9; 3:11; 4:1–3 and 5; 6:1–2; 8:28; 10:6–16 and 12:7, and it is well to recognise this and to keep the artificiality of the construction in mind while reading the book, for then it should be impossible to forget the primary purpose of the narrative, which is not to recount events but to suggest a personal relationship between Yahweh and his people.

## 1 and 2 Samuel

The compilation of various narratives obviously is a factor in the making of these books at least as important as it is in the making of Judges. The present text most forcefully directs attention to a series of doublets in the history; places, that is, where two accounts of the same incident are put side by side, leaving the reader, according to temperament, either puzzled by the disorderliness of the repetition, or delighted at the proffering of a choice as to which he should take. Thus there are two accounts of the rejection of Saul, of David's coming to court, of Saul being in David's power, of David's seeking refuge at Achish, and of Saul's death.

It is also obvious that the material has been put together from various already-existing groupings. Thus our present chapters 1, 3, 4, 7 (7:3–17), 8, 10 (10:17–25), 12 and 15 appear to have been once a continuous narrative into which other pieces of material, including a long section from 9:1 to 10:16, have been set. Whether after or, more probably, before the conflation of the two sources of the first chapters, it seems likely, too, that the story of Samuel was snatched from a collection of material for the history of the judges in order to make an introduction to the royal narratives. Another block of material, chapters 9–20 of 2 Samuel and the first section of 1 Kings, must have been composed by a court scribe during the reign of Solomon.

Of the many later additions to the primitive version of these books it may be proper to point out the account of Samuel foreseeing the tyrannical practices of the future kings and warning Israel against them, for this was probably added by the deuteronomist scribe at almost the last stage of the formation of our present text.

It is important to realise that history was meaningful for the Israelites. They did not think of themselves as living in either an absurd or neutral world. This attitude needs to be explained at some length. We may begin with the title of the books.

These are the 'books of Samuel' not in the sense that Samuel, the seer of Shiloh, wrote down this history (he was dead long before many of the events occurred), but in the sense that he is the major figure of the history. An understanding of his character and actions leads to an understanding of the meaning of the public history. Though Samuel retires into obscurity after the events of the first chapters, he is still the originator of the history. He has brought the other two leading men into public notice, anointing first Saul and then David as king of Israel. His importance as a determining character in the whole narrative is made manifest in the strange episode of the witch of Endor (1 Sam 28:3–25). The ghost of Samuel comes from the rest of the dead to tell the despairing Saul that at the next day's twilight he and his sons will also be mere ghosts. Samuel has made Saul king in Israel, he has warned Saul that Yahweh has rejected him, and at the last comes to tell Saul that this is the end of his rule (28:16 and 19b). To this message a later editor has added the proclamation of the new king (28:17, 18 and 19a), recognising the centrality of the old seer's work in Israelite history.

At the same time most modern readers will be more interested in the characters of the first two kings and the strange ambiguities of judgement in the narratives of Saul and David. It is no easy matter to make for oneself a coherent account of Israelite monarchy. The usual historiographical categories do not apply. The usual judgements do not seem quite to fit.

This perplexity derives from the peculiar character of the society within which the monarchy-traditions formed and were collected. The Israelite tradition had no room for a king. 'Yahweh reigns' was the great cry of the liturgy and the shaping principle of the twelve-tribe alliance. No man could demand the obedience of free Israelites to himself because their obedience was given to Yahweh himself. The men of Israel knew, however obscurely, that it was only in their loyalty to Yahweh that their national unity arose. They were a people because though they had neither blood nor soil in common they believed in the one Lord and were called together by him.

If they neglected Yahweh they would have nothing to keep them together and would either split up into rival groups or become a prey to the neighbourly threats of Egypt or Mesopotamia. This was one element in the Israelite appreciation of political realities. It was balanced by a realisation that while a man was raising his eyes to Yahweh his enemy might steal his vegetables. The realities of Levantine affairs demanded a coordinated and efficient human resistance to the military feudalism of the Sea Peoples (the Philistines, pirates, had settled on the coast of Palestine after their voyage from some Aegean settlement, arriving in Canaan just after the Israelite invaders), and the guerilla warfare of less organised enemies like the Moabites and Amalekites. To be the people of Yahweh they needed a battle leader.

The first answer that the Israelites devised for this problem was, as we have seen, the judge. The Spirit of Yahweh descended upon a man for a particular job. Ehud, Gideon, Barak and Samson are examples of these men of the moment. They rally men for the one task given them, rescue the people from the peril of the hour, and retire. But gradually the Israelites became convinced that their situation demanded a more permanent leadership. Since they were always at war they always needed a battle-leader. Since they were the people of Yahweh the wars they waged were holy wars and he must choose the war-king. The demand of the Israelites for a king and Samuel's reluctance to accede to their demand are both explicable on the Israelite presupposition that they are Yahweh's people.

The growing power of the king (necessitated by the moves to organise the military effort and centralise the economic administration) was the ordinary result of instituting the monarchy. The growing resentment of the people at the royal exactions was the ordinary response of an agricultural population to the press-gang and the tax-collectors. The denunciations of the prophets were not at all ordinary. They were an expression of the peculiar Israelite understanding of life lived under Yahweh.

In these histories, therefore, the kings are seen as splendid men who put on battle-dress and scatter the enemies of Yahweh, often with religious violence that shocks even our over-kill susceptibilities, *and* as brute tyrants who direct labour and conscript infantry with proud disregard of the divine rights of the men of Yahweh. These chronicles are made up from various sources and allow expression to more than one estimate of the monarchy. The famous ambiguities of Samuel's valedictory address are representative of the historian's general attitude towards the kings.

The man who could include in his last working-over of the material both the story of the royal boast of the achievement-column set up after victory *and* the tradition of the old seer's never-ending affection for the handsome warrior had not come to any simple view of Saul.

The man who finally set down both the idyll of the coming shepherd-prince *and* the squalid rape of the mercenary's wife had not come to any simple view of David. And the man who had heard David's royal lament for Saul chanted by some old soldier from the Philistine wars knew that no one else in Israel, not even the kings themselves, had found a simple way to speak to their condition.

So he set down every village tradition he could collect among the country-folk, every cultic yarn of the superstitious priest of the old hill shrines, every formal list of bureaucrats and war-office generals in the national archives, bringing everything to the reader so that the complicated narrative of men's activities should be understood as the movement of Yahweh's will. The great example of a providential description of complicated events is the account of how Solomon became king. This tale of rape and incest, murder and assassination, exile and back-stairs intrigue, which leads to a glory and a wonder beyond the ambition of men, is so deftly told that it is impossible now to separate the various pieces of material brought together by the historian. No later historian has surpassed the narrative skill of this anonymous editor.

At least among near-eastern peoples, the Israelites invented history. Other nations were careful to record the king-list, the battle-honours and the year of foundation stones. But they had no sense of history. Reversewise. For Egyptian and Mesopotamian scribes and their masters a knowledge of the past was required in order to repeat the past. The idea of process was known to them— after all the sun rose upon them and went down on them as well as on the just—but not the idea of progress. There was safety only in carefully repeating what had been done before; if a man did something new who could be sure that the Nile would flood again? For the Egyptian reality was static or at most seasonal, for the Mesopotamian reality was the result of debate among the gods and not governed by any individual will, for the Israelite reality was personal.

If reality is understood as personal then history is developing, for personal relationships develop. History is the working out of Yahweh's personal relationship with his people. History is therefore tellable as a story, a narrative moving onwards.

If history is the unfolding of such a personal relationship then certain categories are ruled out in historical explanation, (categories which suggest that accident or chance are at work), and other categories have to be acknowledged (categories which suggest that plan, responsibility, and punishment and reward are at work). This is the explanation of those strange paragraphs in these narratives which suggest (though not always in a simple manner), that the morality of the performer is the decisive factor in the effectiveness of the performance.

Hophni and Phineas are killed in battle because they have neglected the liturgical worship of Yahweh. David is given victories because he serves Yahweh in humility. It is questionable whether historical explanations dependent upon the assumption of a divine providence are less sophisticated than those explanations which put a total trust in the ubiquity of economic factors or psychological disorders.

At any rate these presuppositions must be acknowledged if 1 and 2 Samuel are to be appreciated. This is the history of Israel, and Israel means 'God reigns'.

## 1 and 2 Kings

The books of Kings seem to have been the first results of the determination of the deuteronomist scribes to write a history of their people which would make plain the meaning of the events they remembered.

The materials these deuteronomist scribes had before them were as diverse as those already suggested as the resources for those who dealt with the history of the judges and of Samuel and the first kings, and they were supplemented by the added evidence obtainable from the royal and temple archives kept in Jerusalem from the time of the aggrandising Solomon. The official court historians, the secretary, or scribe, and the recorder, and their assistants were responsible for an adequate account of the king's great doings, and their responsibility was regarded as sufficiently important for them to be regarded as among the most important officers of state (cf 2 Sam 8:16 ff; 20:24 ff; 1 Kgs 4:2 ff; 2 Kgs 18:18; 2 Chron 34:8).

These officials produced, from the fragmentary information of civil service and army lists, financial records, architects' plans, and sundry other archive materials (cf, eg, 1 Sam 13:1; 2 Sam 5:4f for the kind of information available), historical works which were of some sophistication. Of these works only the name of the *Acts of Solomon* survives (2 Kgs 11:41).

With these old records from the royal archives, which were preserved at the court and kept up to date for the whole monarchical period, those who produced the text we have now had access to the temple archives. They used these, for example, in the accounts of Jehoida's *coup d'état* (2 Kgs 11), and Ahaz' apostasy (2 Kgs 16).

Besides these two sets of official documents the editors placed material from quite a different kind of source. They collected the folk tales of the country dervishes, those sons of the prophets who so enjoyed recounting at their guild meetings the wonders of their heroes. The stories of Elijah (2 Kgs 17–19 and 21 and 2 Kgs 2) are evidently derived by the editors from sources such as these. They have a primitive excitement at the exploits of the holy man much like that which comes across in those camp stories of military song-makers which deal with the pranks of the soldiers' hero, Samson.

The very juxtaposition of such diverse material shows the confidence of the historian in his own culture and in his reader's ability to distinguish the literary and historical form of the narratives as they appeared in the history, and, further, of his reader's ability to make his own judgement about the significance of any part of the chronicle. The editor, that is, trusted the reader to be sensitive enough to know when he should take what was offered him with a pinch of salt.

It is only those who are insensitive to the various modes in which men speak of the fish that got away, their income tax returns, their official attitude to government policy and puss in boots, who find it odd that the men who put together these enlivening histories should be capable of more than one simple attitude and should enjoy more than one form of rhetoric.

Deuteronomy is concerned with the purity of the Jerusalem cult and the rejection of all the Canaanite rituals native to Palestine, and this concern dominates the assessments made by the deuteronomist historian of the kings of Judah and Israel. Of all the kings of Judah only five are said to pass muster, and of these only two, Hezekiah and Josiah, are wholly approved. Of the kings of Israel, after the division of the kingdoms, none is given approval, because each 'walked in the way of Jereboam the son of Nebat', and did not come to worship at the temple in Jerusalem.

In 1 and 2 Kings the final judgement of the historian is always dominated by the liturgical consideration, and is hardly modified by an account of the kings' efforts to deal with political and economic events. This choice of criterion contrasts with the attitude of the davidic court historian of 1 Sam 9 ff who was intensely interested in family and political events as indications of Yahweh's active presence in history as in cult. But the deuteronomist was not so much making a change in Israelite historical writing but rather was re-establishing the old cultic criteria which had been strangely ignored by the court historian. The deuteronomist certainly thought that he was bringing back the decalogue as an historian's proper criterion. From the once-given word of Yahweh in his commandments there goes out a power which may be defied but which inevitably works itself out in events. The historian's task for the people of Yahweh is to make the working of Yahweh's will manifest in past events so that the people will know how to act in the present.

The inevitability of Yahweh's purpose is presented in these books not by accounts of the interplay of character and event but by demonstrating the complementarity of prophecy and fulfilment. It is the deuteronomist who has fixed the popular notion of the prophet as the seer who is given a picture of the inevitable future.

Look, for some examples, at the relation of these few texts:

| *Prophecy* | *Fulfilment* |
| --- | --- |
| 1 Kgs 11:29 ff | 1 Kgs 12:15 |
| 1 Kgs 13 | 2 Kgs 23:16 |
| 1 Kgs 14:6 ff | 1 Kgs 15:29 |
| 1 Kgs 22:17 | 1 Kgs 22:35 ff |
| 2 Kgs 1:6 | 2 Kgs 1:17 |
| 2 Kgs 21:10 | 2 Kgs 24:2 |
| 2 Kgs 22:15 | 2 Kgs 23:30 |

Such complements make the point obvious to the attentive reader. He knows from such patternings precisely what is going on in history and who is in charge and what men are to do.

Of course the work of earlier and minor prophets was more amenable to the deuteronomist's interpretation of events than was that of the greater men. And he knew as well as any modern critic that Elijah, Elisha and Isaiah were not merely seers of future doom but more importantly were urgent reformers of the society in which they lived.

The deuteronomist could accommodate all singular events within the general shape of his history, whether they were prophesied or no. That shape derived from the confrontation of two prophecies which between them accounted for anything that might happen in the kingdoms. The first was that the kingdom of David should not fail, and the second that all should fail who neglected the demand of Yahweh for righteous observance of the Jerusalem cult.

Since God's plan was plain and simple the tortuous process of history must be due to men's interfering with the simple design. History is a history of repeated sin. The history of the kingdoms is seen by the deuteronomist as leading from the sin of Jereboam towards the collapse of the kingdoms in 721 and 586. History is the process in which man unsuccessfully attempts to thwart Yahweh but quite successfully makes himself unhappy. The historian is called to point out how it is that human catastrophe occurs in a world designed by Yahweh.

The deuteronomist thus explains history in terms of sin. The northern kingdom falls because of the original sin of Jereboam 1, and the date of its fall is only delayed by such efforts to serve Yahweh as Ahab's humiliation (1 Kgs 21:29), Jehu's reform (2 Kgs 10:30, 15:12) and Jehoahaz' prayer during the Aramaean raids (2 Kgs 13:23, 14:26). The kings of Israel are brought down because of the deep-seated imperfection in the very being of the kingdom. They are kings of a kingdom which should not be because it has no place in the plan of Yahweh. Their history is the working out of a doom. Judah's history is more complex.

In Judah the promise to Solomon (1 Kgs 11:13) represents a dam against the onrushing power of Yahweh's justice, and this promise of an unfailing line is referred to again and again to explain the otherwise inexplicable survival of the southern kingdom (cf eg, 1 Kgs 11:36, 15:4 and 2 Kgs 8:19). The dynamic interplay of the two theologically certain forces—the retributive will of Yahweh and the love of Yahweh for David—shapes history rough–hew it how we may. Law and love are already in tension in the deuteronomists' account of things as they are.

The tension cannot be resolved even by such a final-seeming catastrophe as the fall of Jerusalem to the heathen in 586. The deuteronomist has still, after this enormous event, a lively faith in the power of divine love, a faith as lively as his belief in divine justice. History therefore remains for ever open to the manifestation of this love.

From the davidic promise there grows an expectation that a king will come who will fulfil the demands of Yahweh to the full, such a king will be the fulfilment of all prophecy, he will put an end to the cause of Yahweh's anger and inaugurate a kingdom of love. The notion of history that the deuteronomist entertains is, therefore, open to a messianic interpretation, but of the messiah he knows nothing concrete, he has simply to recount what has happened from the time of David to his own. He begins therefore with the testament of the old king in Jerusalem.

*1. How is it possible for anyone today to advance a theory of history when we are so aware of the higgledy-piggledy in our lives?*

*2. Is it at all profitable to relate the Hebrew understanding of prophecy to the present interest in newspaper horoscopes which seem so often to say something quite apposite to our lives?*

*3. If history is thought to have a purpose is the scope of human freedom necessarily restricted?*

## Book list for Judges, 1 & 2 Samuel, 1 & 2 Kings

G. F. Moore, *Judges*, Edinburgh, 1949.

E. C. Rust, *Judges, Ruth, and 1 and 2 Samuel*, London, 1961.

H. W. Hertzberg, *1 and 2 Samuel*, London 1964.

W. McKane, *1 and 2 Samuel*, London 1963.

J. A. Montgomery, *1 and 2 Kings*, Edinburgh 1951.

J. Gray, *1 and 2 Kings*, London 1963.

H. F. G. Swanston, *The Kings and the Covenant*, London 1967.

G. Robinson, *Historians of Israel* (*1*), London 1962.

E. W. Heaton, *The Hebrew Kingdoms*, Oxford 1969.

# Judges

# 1

# The first judges
# Jgs 1:1–5:31

**Jgs 1:1–3:6. Introduction**

**Jgs 1:1.** This introductory verse attempts to make the story continuous with the book of Joshua, as Josh 1:1 links that book with the Pentateuch. But it is evident that there is some overlapping (cf, eg, Josh 15:13–19 and 63 with Jgs 1:10 and 21).

History is here thought to be linear, one thing happens after another and should therefore be written down in straight-line sequence. The Hebrews were somewhat ashamed of what now appears to us a virtue: their capacity to look at events in more than one way. The conquest of Canaan was both a series of bloody attacks on stoutly defended townships, and a sign of Yahweh's invincible progress through the land; cf Josh 10:28 ff and Jgs 1:3 ff.

**Jgs 1:3.** Judah and Simeon are personifications of particularly close tribal allies, for they are sons not only of one father but of one mother, cf Gen 35:23.

**Jgs 1:15.** The story is told to explain the claim of Achsah, a branch of the Kenizzite clan Othniel of Debir, to waters which by their situation seemed naturally to belong to the older line, the Calebites of Hebron, cf Josh 15:17 ff.

**Jgs 1:28 ff.** From earliest times to those of the building of the Suez Canal the corvee was used in the Near East for public works, cf Kgs 9:22, 12:4 and 18. The historian is accounting for the presence of so many pagans in the tribal territories after the conquest, and preparing for the sad story of pagan cultic influences in Israel's later history.

*1. The Hebrews evidently required traditional origins for their present way of life, and thus concocted stories to account for the names of places they inhabited. Is tradition important for us to understand our lives?*

*2. Do we, in these days of the* UN *and the Common Market, have any great need to keep up our patriotic feelings?*

**Jgs 2:1–3.** The messenger of Yahweh seems to have been here, as elsewhere, cf Jgs 6:8 ff, a wandering seer with but one moment of inspiration recorded by the historian, who evidently did not know the seer's name. The man of Yahweh voices, of course, the later deuteronomic thesis of a causal link between Hebrew allowance of, and even participation in, the foreign cults in the holy land and the misfortunes of the later kingdoms.

This incident serves, like many another in Judges, to account for the later name of the place. *Bochim* means *Weepers* and the shrine there became the great sanctuary of Bethel.

### Jgs 3:12–30. Ehud

Early in the twelfth century the men of Moab defeated the tribe of Reuben and began to encroach upon the Benjamite lands across the Jordan. The tribute of the cowering Benjamites was brought each year to Eglon of

Moab, either at his home, or at his army headquarters when he was on the march.

The year Ehud carried the tribute money to Eglon at his residence east of the Jordan the Moabite was tricked by the left-handed Benjamite into allowing him to approach at a private audience, and was assassinated. The story of the fat king's death is told with some literary skill and an amount of relish. Left-handed Benjamites are remarked in the later story of the Gibeah outrage, Jgs 20:16.

The wholly Benjamite character of Ehud's revolt may be discerned at 3:28 ff, for the tribes make no effort to assist their Reuben kinsmen on the other side of the Jordan. They are concerned only with what happens on their side of the fording places.

**Jgs 3:19.** After the magical elements of the left-hander and the killing of the Moabite beast in his secret den, the narrative places the sacred stones—rather as in the epic story of Gilgamesh, with which he and his readers were certainly acquainted, the uselessness of Enkidu's right hand and the slaying of the monster Humbaba in his fastness is followed by Gilgamesh's rushing past the sacred stones on his way to the magic river. Are these the stones set up by Joshua, cf Josh 4:20, or boundary stones which, when passed, gave Ehud the assurance that he was back in Israelite territory and could safely proclaim a tribal revolt?

## Jgs 4:4–5:31. Deborah and Barak

The great poem of chapter 5 is probably contemporary with the events it describes, and seems to be the oldest piece of historical writing we possess. It is certainly written before chapter 4.

It appears that the Galilean tribes were subject to the rule of Sisera's army of warrior Philistines and pressed native Canaanite troops from the plains of Esdraelon and Acco, and that they appealed for help to the independent tribe of Naphtali and its soldier Barak. Barak has no official status in the tribe, he is simply the man for the moment chosen by Yahweh as an instrument in the holy war of liberation from pagan dominion.

The plan of campaign in a holy war was to consult the oracle of Yahweh, follow the divine instruction and then offer the captured booty to Yahweh. There could be no ransoming of prisoners, for example, when they were Yahweh's enemies.

Barak's troops, having consecrated themselves on the holy Mount Tabor, were able to defeat a chariot force for the first time because Yahweh sent rain enough to clog the Philistines' chariot wheels on the plain of Jezreel, cf 5:4 and 21.

**Jgs 4:11.** *The Kenites* often puzzled the Hebrew historians. They were not of the tribal confederacy and yet they had helped Judah at the conquest; they were not Hebrews and yet Moses had married a daughter of one of their priests and accepted his cult—cf Num 10:29 ff. This Kenite evidently had wandered from his tribe and its tents in the region south of Judah.

Among bedouin it was the women's task to pitch tent, but there is no reason to suppose that Jael would not have seen that the quickest way with Sisera would be to dash his brains out with the mallet. The description of the killing in 5:26, from which the later 4:21 derives, is really a piece of Hebrew parallelism. She did not use two instruments when one would do.

**Jgs 5:28.** The description of the pagan lady at the

window suggests a comparison with the Egyptian custom of granting audiences from a balcony, and other royal appearances at pagan windows, cf Abimelech of Philistia, Gen 26:8, and Jezebel of Tyre, 2 Kgs 9:30 ff.

*1. The stories of Ehud, the odd man out because of his left-handedness, and of Deborah, the woman in a man's world, shew that Yahweh can employ the most unlikely persons to achieve the good of the whole community. What thoughts does this suggest to those of us who wonder whether our small individual effort can be worth much?*

*2. Does the evident bloodthirstiness of these tales lessen their usefulness in our society, now that we are concerned with how to live at peace?*

# 2
## Gideon
## Jgs 6:11–8:32

The confederation of Israelite townships and villages of the plain of Esdraelon collapsed at the attacks of Midianite raiders. These nomads of the desert brought a new terror to warfare: the camel. Riding these horrific beasts the Midianites came at threshing time and carried away the grain, and no man seemed able to stop them.

This story is the great holy war saga. It is recounted in such a way that no one will ascribe the victory to any but Yahweh. The hero is evidently a passive instrument, and his army purposely small in order that the divine effect may be the more evident. The men are called upon to do little more than take up symbolic positions, they are priests of the liturgy with trumpets blowing and lights lit for the ceremony of victory, best likened to the priestly celebrants at the fall of Jericho, Josh 6:15 ff.

**Jgs 6:11.** There is an interest for christian readers in the form of the conversation between Gideon and the angel announcing the divine plan of salvation for his people. Evidently Luke saw Gideon as a precursor of Mary in the divine work and took the literary shape of his annunciation narrative from this story, cf Jgs 6–12 f and Lk 1:28 f.

Two versions of the call of Gideon and building of the altar have been conflated in 6:11–24 and 25–32.

**Jgs 6:25.** The post is the asherah of Ex 34:14, Deut 12:3 et al.

**Jgs 6:31.** Joash thinks Baal must be able to defend himself and this belief allows the author some literary irony in the telling of the tale.

**Jgs 7:8.** Those who leave give their food and trumpets to those who stay.

**Jgs 7:16–22.** Two accounts have been conflated here, one dealt with jars and torches, the other with horns.

**Jgs 8:16.** The men are threshed together with thistles.

**Jgs 8:20.** For the boy it was an honour to avenge his uncles who had been killed in their homes, for the kings it was a shaming disregard of their manhood.

**Jgs 8:24–7.** The ephod mentioned here is an oracular idol, cf 17:5 and 18:14 and Hos 3:4; it is not the later priestly vestment.

**Jgs 8:33–35.** These verses were once meant as a substitute for chapter 9 which, having been deleted by the deuteronomist, was restored later and these verses survived the restoration of that for which they had substituted.

The total agency of Yahweh in the victory is emphasised in Gideon's refusal to become a king among Yahweh's own people, 8:23; cf Hos 13:10, and later in the bitterly anti-monarchic parable of Jotham, 9:7–15. This sarcastic tale starts from the conviction that if a man is any good at any other job he will not want to be a king, and ends in a picture of a king as one who is full of boasts that he cannot fulfil—the idea of the bramble sheltering the other trees is nonsensical—and of threats of violence

that he knows only too well how to implement. This
proper horror of kingship is manifest also in 1 Sam 12:6 ff;
2 Sam 24 and 1 Kgs 11:29 ff.

Like other of the histories in the old testament this
story of Gideon has elements of folk and fairy tale and
heroic saga. The useless man who entertains a wondrous
being unawares and is rewarded is related to Cinderella,
he who slays the seven year-old bullock and is given a
strange fleece has something in common with Jason, and
he who gains a magic victory after a dream, slays seventy-
seven princes and is rewarded with a hoard of golden
rings is kin to Siegfried. And very pleasing it is to discover
how rich and allusive are these narratives when they
seem at first so straightforward and uninteresting. There
is perhaps a conflation, in the present text of chapters
6–9, of two heroic tales, one of Gideon and the other of
Jerubbaal, but there is not a great hope of disentangling
them now.

**Jgs 9.** The story of Abimelech, the son of Jerubbaal, is
evidently one which depends for its motive power upon
the uneasy relations of the Hebrew tribesmen and the
original Canaanite inhabitants of the land.

Abimelech appeals to his Canaanite relations to help
him overthrow the members of his father's family who
rule Shechem from the tribal citadel of Ophrah. His
revolt succeeds but after a while the Canaanites resent
the rule of the half-breed and accept the brigand Gaal as
their leader at a fertility festival when their spirits are
cheerful.

Abimelech's officer gives him intelligence of these
events and the insurrection is crushed by sword and fire
at Shechem, and at the bolt-hole fortress of Thebez,
though Abimelech himself is killed at the moment of

victory. Jotham's curse on both people and king is fulfilled.

*1. The story of Gideon suggests a unity of liturgical and social action. The two come together to bring about the victory of good in the society. How are we to bring our liturgical worship and our social concern into practical harmony?*

*2. Does it matter for the effectiveness of whatever lesson we get from the story of Gideon, that we are sceptical about its reliability as an historical narrative?*

# 3

# Jephthah and others
# Jgs 10:1–12:15

**Jgs 10:1–3.** These two judges come from yet other tribes. Ehud was a Benjamite, Barak a man of Naphtali, Gideon of a clan of Manasseh, now Tola is of Issachar and later Elon is of Zebulon. Jair, Ibzan and Abdan certainly and others perhaps, are really clan names representing power changes in the confederacy.

**Jgs 10:4.** For the importance of riding on asses, cf 12:14 and other Hebrew accounts of princes and kings up to the Palm Sunday entrance of Jesus to Jerusalem.

The historian knew nothing of Jephthah's origins, cf 11:8, and supplied a plausible conjecture which allows him to present a happy twist of events: the despised man becomes the cheered hero.

**Jgs 11:11 ff.** There seems to be an oath-taking before the people at Yahweh's sanctuary, which leads into a recital of the exodus wonder, and a renewal of the sense of a people chosen to rule in Palestine.

**Jgs 11:30.** The vow story may be compared to the tale of Agamemnon and Iphigeneia, especially as told in the *Iphigeneia in Tauris,* and to the tale of Idomeneo, cf *Aeneid* 3.121; 9.264. This seems to have been a very old story with which the later historian could not tamper but which he may have sensed belonged with the pagan rituals of those who wept for Tammuz and he made efforts to relate it to Hebrew ritual.

**Jgs 12:1 ff.** It would almost appear from this episode and the parallel passage in Jgs 8:1 ff that the men of Ephraim were accustomed to make a living from pillage and from grabbing the booty taken by other tribes in fights with the Canaanites. This time they cannot frighten their way into success, as they had when Gideon was a judge, and they get their come-uppance.

**Jgs 12:8.** Another judge from another tribe of whom the name and nothing more was known to the historian.

*1. The incident of Jephthah and his daughter reminds us of the processes by which Israel absorbed other religious traditions into its general account of the world. What features of what other religious traditions besides those of judaism—Zen, for instance— might christians consider taking into their system?*

*2. Are vows to God generally dangerous things to make? Ought they to be regarded more like promises to men which every- one understands cannot always be kept?*

# 4

# Samson
# Jgs 13:1–16:31

Samson, unlike the other judges, is a solitary hero who fights alone against Yahweh's enemies. There is no trace of the deuteronomist's editorial work in this section. We are presented with a simple folk-tale of very doubtful historicity.

**Jgs 13:1 ff.** The story of Samson's birth should be compared with other stories of long-barren women, cf Sam 1:2 and Lk 1:7. The annunciation story is much like that of the Gideon story, and perhaps is the work of the same author.

**Jgs 13:19.** The cereal oblation is added here and at 13:23 for the sake of liturgical correctness.

**Jgs 13:20.** Cf Gideon story, 6:21.

**Jgs 13:24.** *Samson* is derived from *shemesh* or *sun*— Bethshemesh, a village just across the valley from Manoah's home, was sacred to the sun-god. Perhaps this Israelite story has its origins in a sun god's ritual.

**Jgs 13:25.** Here it would appear that we have the introduction to some lost first story of Samson. In all the extant stories Samson has a just occasion for his fight and revenges against the rascally men of Philistia.

**Jgs 14:5a and 6b.** Samson's father and mother are brought into the narrative by a later editor lest it be surmised that Samson contracted a marriage with an alien against his parents' will. The bridegroom's men are young Philistines and not members of his family.

If we take it that 14:5a and 6b, and 10a, are not part of the original story we have a clearer account of Samson's journeys to Timnah during his courtship and, their union not being a full marriage, we can understand both Samson's treatment of the girl and her father's supposition that he can marry her off to someone else. Samson's taking a kid on his visit to her, 15:1, suggests that the girl had to be paid for her services and was never thought to be his true wife. The father was obviously a bad lot and prepared to trade in another daughter, 15:2.

**Jgs 14:19.** The story of the killing of the men of Ashkelon is interpolated here so that Samson shall never be seen to have been thwarted by the wicked foreigner. It is an incident which, unlike every other tale in this collection of heroic narratives, has no consequence. It is certainly added at a late stage of the telling.

**Jgs 15:4.** This is a rip-roaring tale which is not meant to be taken literally.

**Jgs 15:11.** In Judah Samson seemed merely a stranger who had made trouble. This is a further sidelong piece of evidence that the tribes had not yet discovered the meaning of their confederation.

**Jgs 16:1.** The Gaza episode must have been part of a very old story for the historian is forced to follow a tale of his hero's careless attitude towards marriage and wantonness with a foreigner with another like unto it.

**Jgs 16:4 ff.** The Delilah story is a typically robust piece of folk-narrative. We are to watch wiliness opposed to wiliness. Evidently Delilah calls out her warning that the Philistines are upon Samson as a test to try if his bonds were really strong enough to hold him. The Philistines do not come from their hiding place until it is certain that Samson is strengthless.

**Jgs 16:27.** If the 3000 on the roof are an addition to the original tale it is clearer how the house of the notable rested upon two pillars. The author is to be allowed his patriotic exaggeration here as elsewhere.

**Jgs 16:28.** Samson's 'judging' amounts to no more than a set of folktale adventures which set going a line of saga recitals of his legend. He is rather like Herakles. Perhaps the whole narrative is a camp story told when the men of Saul waited to fight the Philistine army and needed some reassurance that an Israelite had beaten these pagans before.

Several incidents in the story of Samson seem to belong with the mysterious folk-origins of other tales and to express certain primitive proprieties. The solving of the riddle on the seventh day may suggest to us the Theban Sphinx and Rumpelstiltskin, and the three attempts to find the truth of Samson's secret strength may remind us of such questions as 'Who's been sleeping in my bed?' and such boastings as 'I'll huff and I'll puff and I'll blow your house down'.

It is possible too that the seduction of the strong man by the foreign temptress, and the carrying away of the gates of the city are related almost directly to some original tale which inspired in the epic of Gilgamesh the incident of Enkidu's seduction by the temple whore of Erek when his strength is much diminished and his animal vigour sapped, and the incident in the same story of Enkidu's fight at the door with Gilgamesh when the bride is waiting for her husband.

And perhaps, again, the gouging out of Samson's eyes is related to his sins against the sexual customs of his country. His seeking a foreign girl instead of choosing from the Hebrew village maidens may have brought down on him a punishment that fitted the crimes of Oedipus and of Gloucester in *King Lear*.

*1. The stories of Ehud and of Deborah shewed how Yahweh can employ any man, the final scene of the story of Samson shews how Yahweh can bring something out of the worst mess men make of their lives. How are we to recognise the causes for hope in our lives?*

*2. What tales do we use in our society now to cheer ourselves?*

# 5

# The shrine of Dan
# Jgs 17:1–18:31

**Jgs 17:1.** This a story from two hands. The present editor has put together two strands of the narrative so that he has a fuller account of the origins of the great northern shrine of Dan.

**Jgs 17:3.** The intention of the dedication of the money is not to devote the total treasure to Yahweh's use or to the making of an image, but to render the money taboo until the woman had made an image from part of it.

**Jgs 17:4.** Despite the use of 'graven image' here, there is no suggestion that the editor disapproves of the woman's intention.

**Jgs 17:5.** The ephod here may have been an idol but one cannot be certain. The only surety we have in describing this object is that it was used by the priest in consulting the oracle. The teraphim are idols generally associated with Canaanite shrines, cf Gen 31:19, Jgs 18:24 and Hos 3:4. There is a general haziness, therefore, in the editor's mind about what Micah's shrine actually contained, cf 18:14 and 17.

**Jgs 17:6.** This reference seems to suggest a lawless time but it may simply be reasserting the historical context in order that the reader has some anchor in the turmoil of events, cf 18:1. The emphasis in the telling is on the uncertain state of society in which a son steals from his mother, a levite has no home, and a Hebrew tribe is still living a nomadic existence.

**Jgs 18:22–6.** Cf Laban's pursuit of Jacob, Gen 31:22. This is a quietly written account of this pathetic incident which brings out the unhappiness involved in the origins of the shrine.

**Jgs 18:30.** There is a reference here to the deportations carried out by Tiglath-pileser in 734, cf 2 Kgs 15:29.

**Jgs 18:31.** This story of the origin of the Dan shrine should be coupled with the shorter account of the origin of the Bethel shrine, 2:1 ff. Both are older sancturies than the davidic shrine in Jerusalem and have historic claims to be the traditional shrines of the Hebrew people.

*1. What is wrong with having an idol as the image of the unseen?*

*2. What do we mean when we say that man is 'the image of God'?*

*3. Ought we always to keep our attention on the visible, tasteable, tangible world about us or is there a use in thinking of the unknown other world beyond us?*

# 6

# The outrage of Gibeah
# Jgs 19:1—21:25

**Jgs 19:1 ff.** This is most obviously of all the stories in Judges a piece of inventive history. Whatever incident lies behind the story we now have, it was written to persuade the Hebrews that their tribal unity was strong and effective at a time when no one attached any importance to the confederation.

The teller of this tale has taken some ideas from other Hebrew stories, for example, the girl being used to protect the levite reminds the reader of the story of Abraham and Sarai in Gen 12 and of the Sodom story, Gen 19:8, but generally the teller has relied upon his own literary skill to construct a patriotic tale.

The important factor in this brilliantly told story is not the fate of the poor girl, as it certainly would be in any modern telling, but the fate of the tribal confederacy. Every incident is related to the importance of the tribal society when 'there was no king in Israel'. The note of a tribal time begins, 19:1, and ends, 21:25, the narrative:

(a) The events take place in Gibeah precisely because the levite will not spend a night in the city of foreigners, 19:12.
(b) The old man comes, like the levite, from the hill country of Ephraim, 19:16 and 19:1, and the fault

of the Benjamites begins with their ignoring the plight of a Hebrew in the square.

(c) The Benjamite fellows act like the men of Sodom, Gen 19:5 f and Jgs 19:22 ff, and thus indicate that they have no care of the covenant society.

(d) After the rape the levite appeals to tribal loyalties in just the way Saul employs, cf 1 Sam 11:7.

(e) The matter is brought before 'all the people' acting as a covenant congregation at Mizpah, cf Jgs 10:17.

(f) The levite appeals to the assembly as a people able to act together and bearing corporate responsibility for the style of life that the covenant enjoins, 20:7.

(g) The people make their decision in terms of the Exodus journey and the principles of conduct that they there received, 20:8, and they fully expect the Benjamites to respect the same confederate principles, 20:13.

(h) The war council of the tribes takes place at Bethel 'for the ark of the covenant was there in those days', 20:27.

(i) The model upon which the fight is planned and narrated is that of the holy war:

Day 1   The Benjamites kill 22,000 men and lose none at all: there follows a vigil of prayer;

Day 2   the Benjamites kill 18,000 men and lose none: there follows a second vigil of prayer;

Day 3   Israel kills 25,100 men at the fight and loses 30: only 600 Benjamites remain at Rimmon.

Evidently this is not intended as a literal narrative of battles but as a schematic account of how after two days of defeat and prayer on the third day the victory was given to those who remained true to the covenant.

The account appears to be a midrashic elaboration of some scribe who belonged to the group who produced the books of Chronicles. The tone is quite unlike the rest of Judges.

(j) The oath at Mizpah, which is suddenly introduced here in order that the narrator may have another opportunity to stress the importance of the covenant among the tribes, looks as if there must be an end of one of the tribes in the confederation, and thus the end of the confederation itself, for without one tribe the others are not fully themselves. This crisis brings the people back to the shrine at Bethel with a determination to find some way of preserving the covenant confederacy.

(k) The story is rounded off by the return of all the tribes to the territories they were believed to have been given at the conquest, 21:24.

**Jgs 21:1 ff.** The repetitions in this chapter, after the general cultic setting has been declared, 21:1–4, of the questions in verses 5a and 8, 7 and 16, and of the description of the tribal predicament, 5b and 18b, lead into a second cultic situation, verses 19–24. This suggests that some ancient Canaanite harvest ceremony with its fertility associations has been incorporated into Hebrew culture by the simple device of making it commemorative of an incident in the covenant history (cf the story of the Jephtha.) The cult and the history are united in this final editing of the primitive tale.

*1. Why were fertility rites so popular in the ancient world? What are their equivalents in our world?*

*2. Does the Judges history as a whole make it clear why the Hebrews began to look for a central permanent authority for their state?*

# 1 and 2 Samuel

# 1

# The boy Samuel
# 1 Sam 1:1–3:21

**1 Sam 1:1–2:10. The boy is born**

**1 Sam 1:1–3.** The story of the kings begins in the liturgy. Elkanah brings his wives to Shiloh, the shrine of the ark, and sacrifices at the annual feast of the tribes at the beginning of the year (in the first days of autumn). The barren woman has come to understand that nothing can come of the flesh except by the power of Yahweh (cf Gen 18:14; Lk 1:36; Rom 4:19–21; Heb 11:11); worn out by the taunts of Elkanah's other and fruitful wife, Hannah prays at the pilgrimage centre for divine compassion.

**1 Sam 1:4–7.** The high moment of the pilgrimage comes at the sacrificial feast, and many of those who joined in the celebration must have got drunk. Eli's mistake is understandable.

**1 Sam 1:7–18.** Hannah's reply suggests a comparison with Luke's account of the visitation when God is said to have regarded the low condition of his servant. On this occasion too the woman is speaking of her being given her first-born son.

**1 Sam 1:19–20.** The boy is called Samuel, evidently from *shem* (name) and *'el*, (God), and probably Samuel should be understood as 'the boy born through the power of God' since 'name' is often used in both old and new testaments for 'power', for example, the first christians are described in Acts as baptising 'in the name of Jesus' (Acts 2:38). Samuel is in his own person a sign that God is at work among his people.

The narrator has made a real effort to place 'the man of God' in the centre of the action from the beginning of his story. It is just possible that he had to elbow aside the figure of the first king to achieve this purpose. The boy born to Hannah is repeatedly said to be born only because she asked God for a son, and 'Samuel' is said to mean 'I have asked for him from the Lord'. The root of the word *saal*, ask, is much more like *saul* than *semuel*, and 'saul' means 'he who is asked for'. A play on this word occurs in verses 27–28. The same root is at the base of 'ask' and 'lend', so the child asked *is* the child lent, both are *saul*. It is therefore likely that the story of Hannah was originally a story of Saul's birth, a royal tale current among courtiers and not at all to do with the priestly circles among which Samuel was brought up. The editor of the material may well have shifted the reference of the story in order to make it obvious that it was not the king but the judge who was sent by God at the asking of the oppressed people.

**1 Sam 2:1–11.** The psalm is an insertion, probably because of the 'barren woman' in verse 5, as can be seen in the immediate sequence of verse 2:11a from verse 1:28b. The occurrence of a psalm from the cultic celebration of Yahweh's saving holiness in this narrative shows that the editor is doing everything he can to emphasise the liturgical setting of Samuel's infancy. The work of the great man begins in the sacral sphere.

Christian readers have sometimes thought it of interest that some of the phrases in this psalm occur again in the *Magnificat* (2:1; cf Lk 1:46: 2:8; cf Lk 1:52), but the generalised tone of this psalm is not quite that of the personal exultation of the *Magnificat*, and if any particular old testament source is used in the lukan narrative, it would seem much more likely to be found in a later passage in 2 Samuel, (6:11 ff).

*1. Are there any justifying reasons for re-writing history in order to speak to contemporary conditions?*

*2. Can history be written any other way?*

## 1 Sam 2:11–3:21. Life in the sanctuary

**1 Sam 2:11.** The intention of the editor of this passage is evidently to make a vivid contrast between the worthless and spoilt sons of Eli and the young Samuel quietly serving God in the liturgy of the sanctuary. Samuel from the beginning stands out as resisting any human corruption. He has no part at all in the sacrileges of Hophni and Phineas.

The laymen coming up to the shrine intending to offer the proper sacrifice to God are shewn to be better than the professional priests (2:16), so the editor was evidently not making a crude pro-clerical statement when he singled out Samuel rather than Saul as the hero of his history. Quite the contrary. One point of the opening narrative is to emphasise that Samuel does not belong to the hereditary priestly families. He is a new man, given by God, who by his presence shows up the uselessness of the official leaders. The significance of Samuel as opposed to the old priesthood is a complement to his significance as opposed to the new kings. He is the last of the judges and lives a life very like that described of the earlier leadership, he performs the priestly functions, but he is equally the first of the prophets.

**1 Sam 2:18.** The loin-cloth Samuel wears seems to be a sign of his complex vocation. The linen cloth is called an *ephod*. This word is certainly used for the priestly garment, but it does not have a wholly priestly connotation: King David, for example, wore the *ephod* when he brought the ark into Jerusalem (2 Sam 6:14). Samuel thus wears the *ephod* as a sign that he has a service to perform for the Lord, but it is not a service limited by priestly functions. Over the *ephod* the young boy wore a tunic which may be a sign of capacity to rule others (cf Is 3:6), or of a prophetic office (cf 2 Kgs 2:13), or simply to keep him warm.

Up to this time Samuel has been not entirely in the care of Yahweh, his mother has had responsibility for his clothing, but now Yahweh takes Samuel for his total service and so Hannah is given other children (2:21) and does not appear in the story again. Samuel belongs wholly to Yahweh.

**1 Sam 2:25–26.** The contrasts between the priests and boy are built up throughout this chapter. Hophni and Phineas pay no attention to Eli, Samuel grows in favour with men; Hophni and Phineas drive Yahweh to determine on their deaths, Samuel grows in favour with Yahweh. In 2:29 the indulgent Eli is said to think more of his sons than he does of Yahweh and so all the named members of the priestly order are implicated in their sin. In 2:32 every priest is incriminated and included in the punishment: they will all die before they are old men. The promise of one man of the house being left to do the priestly office probably refers to the escape of Abiathar

from the slaughter of the priests by Saul (1 Sam 22:20).
He lived to be the chief priest and then through his own
folly to be exiled from Solomon's court (1 Kgs 2:26).
The prophecy of a new priesthood serving before the
anointed king is a reference to the rise of the Zadokite
family (1 Sam 8–17).

**1 Sam 3:1.** This is brought out at the beginning of the
next chapter, where in a narrative derived from another
source, both the manner of Samuel's experience and its
content are signs of Yahweh's rejection of the priests. It is
explicitly stated that 'it was rare for Yahweh to speak in
those days' (3:1), that the call did not come through the
official priestly channels (3:5 and 6) and that Yahweh,
when he does speak, gives his word of condemnation for
the priests (3:11–14).

Samuel's response to the call, 'Here I am', puts him
along with Abraham (Gen 22:1), and Jacob (Gen 31:11;
46:2), it is the response too of Isaiah (Is 6:9) and, in the
new testament, of the prophet Ananias (Acts 9:10).
Samuel is 'ready to hear' and he is now himself the
occasion of Yahweh's coming to the shrine. The man has
eclipsed the ark. 'Samuel grew up and Yahweh was with
him.'

**1 Sam 3:19.** Everything is handed over to Samuel.
Yahweh comes continually to him and the people recognise him to be a prophet, from the northern shrine of
Dan to the southern Beersheba. The contrast between the
barren flesh and the quickening power of the word of God
is complete.

*1. Is the judge a better model for the christian leader than the
high priest?*

*2. What is to be thought of the predominance of liturgical
matters in this description of God's will for his people?*

# 2
# The loss of the ark
# 1 Sam 4:1–7:3

**1 Sam 4:1.** At this point the editor presents a piece of material totally distinct in origin from the Shiloh tradition of the first chapters. Although there are certain incongruities between the two traditions, the new material allows the editor to introduce both the ark and the Philistines.

The ark is the centralising sign of Yahweh's presence among the disparate tribes for it is the chest in which are kept the tablets recording the covenant bond of Yahweh and his people, and it is also the throne of Yahweh. It is highly unlikely that each of the tribes was represented in the Hebrews gathered at Sinai on the desert journey, yet all the tribes had accepted a share in the covenant and had joined in the covenant confederation of Yahweh's people, all had given their loyalty to the society signified in the ark of the covenant. Shiloh was the shrine to which men like Elkanah came because there the ark was.

Remembrance of the heroic stories of the conquest of Canaan by Joshua and his men led the Hebrews to suppose that wherever the ark went the presence of Yahweh was bound to bring victory. After a severe defeat in the northern territory the Hebrews determined to bring the ark into the battle line.

Their war is against the Philistines. These were a

people who came probably from round the walls of Troy, had certainly spent some time in Crete, and now occupied a coastal strip of land and the five great towns of Gaza, Ashkelon, Ashdod, Ekron and Gath. These formed a feudal aristocracy maintained by an interdependent group of military garrisons which could turn out as a united army whenever any one town was threatened by attack from the native Canaanite population or the other, Hebrew, invaders of the land.

At Aphek, the Philistines also remember the exodus and the conquest. They are terrified at the coming of the Lord of battles to the front. Determined not to disgrace themselves, they stiffen their sinews, summon up their blood and cry havoc. They win.

The last remnant of the army of Israel is routed, Hophni and Phineas are killed, the ark itself is captured. On being told the news Eli falls backward off his stool at the entrance to the empty shrine.

The Philistines drive onward and destroy the sanctuary of Shiloh. Everything is now in turmoil. The public horror of the loss of the ark and the death of the great priest who has ruled for an age, is reflected in the private upheaval of Phineas' wife. The pains of giving birth force her to 'turn over and over' (the same word is used of the destruction of Sodom and Gomorrah), and the child Ichabod, whose name signifies the loss of the ark, is born into a family of the dead.

**1 Sam 5:1.** In bawdy contrast to this stark tragedy the editor has put some coarse stories of what happens to the uncircumcised when they grab the ark of Yahweh. Their gods fall down and lose their heads. Dagon has to be picked up like a fallen child and put back upright in his place. Funnier still, Yahweh 'strikes them on their behinds' and brings out sores on every anus in Ashdod. The editor becomes quite boisterous in his telling of how the men of Ashdod pass on the ark to Gath like a hot brick and when these are afflicted in like manner, the ark is hurried off to Ekron and as the sores break out there too, Yahweh is seen to triumph over every enemy. Those who thought they could manage him as they had managed the men of Israel had a rude shock. 'The wailing from the town went up to heaven'. They admit defeat.

**1 Sam 6:1.** The editor now pictures a hurried council of the magicians and diviners of the heathen. Their open admission of a defeat in parallel with that of Egypt is the last satisfaction his audience would require. Yahweh has vindicated himself.

The ark is returned and the liturgy is performed again. Levites spring from nowhere and the normal order is restored with proper sacrifice and ceremonial correctness before the distant eyes of the gentile princes who dare not intrude on the Hebrew ritual. So important is it that everything should be done according to form and custom that seventy Hebrews are struck dead for not taking their proper part in the service of thanksgiving.

At the end of the narrative the ark waits at Kiriath-Jearim for the anointed king to bring it ceremoniously into the capital of the new empire. The editor has to turn to other strands of his history so that he can later present the convergence of the divine purposes in the royal shrine of Jerusalem.

*1. Why do you think the journey of the ark from the great northern shrine of Shiloh down (eventually) to the new southern capital of Jerusalem was important to the editor?*

*2. Do you have much sympathy for 'symbolic' episodes, such as the birth of Ichabod or the Philistine's boils, so common in the bible?*

# 3

# Samuel the judge
# 1 Sam 7:4–12:25

**A. 1 Sam 7:3–7:14. The battle of Mizpah**
**1 Sam 7:3.** The defeat of Israel at Aphek is ascribed not to their lack of military science but to their apostate worship of the Ashtaroth fertility idols and the Baal gods of the foreigner. If they are to recover their lost nationality and become again the people of Yahweh, they must have a change of heart (cf Joel 3:21), and turn to Yahweh.

**1 Sam 7:5.** Samuel performs a confession ritual at the hill sanctuary of Mizpah (cf Jer 40:1 Macc 3), and there pours out water as a sign of the people weeping not for Tammuz or Osiris but in repentance for sin (cf Lam 2:19). Samuel is here seen as the prophet who calls the people to turn again, as the priest who offers intercession and sacrifice on behalf of the people, and as judge. The complexity and importance of Samuel's functions and personality are again emphasised.

**1 Sam 7:7.** The Philistines, who evidently had good grounds for supposing the Israelites to be finished, on hearing of the assembly at Mizpah take it to be a threat to their rule.

The Israelites have learnt the lesson of Aphek, they neither attempt to rally their own forces against the superior military strength of the Philistines, nor to thrust Yahweh, whether he will or no, into the fight. They ask

Samuel to intercede for them. The divine answer comes (cf Jos 6; 10:13; Jgs 5:10). Yahweh himself routs the enemy. The men of Israel have only to engage in mopping-up operations. The theology of war of this narrative is much more important to the editor than any historical account of what actually happened. No better example of the 'holy war' could be framed since the Israelite army is not engaged at all in the fighting and has no share of the glory. This is the meaning of the erection of the monument (7:12).

## B. 1 Sam 8:1–8:22. The demand for a king

Samuel's sons, like those of Gideon and Eli, are not the men their father was. They take bribes in the law courts. The people demand that some settled way of government is given them which will not depend so entirely on the personality and talents of the leader.

To the editor it is evident that the people in asking for a king are inviting trouble, they are degrading themselves to the level of the heathen and running the risk of further apostasy from the service of the one Lord Yahweh. At the same time the risk must be taken. The growth of the nation demands a change of the national institutions. Yahweh gives Israel a king. The narrative therefore is the first indication in the text of the anointed king as the man sent by Yahweh to the people.

The account of Samuel's speech to the people is shaped by the ambiguity of the situation. Samuel warns the people of the autocratic heathen ways that are common to a king and of the great difference there will be between their oppression by foreign kings and their oppression by their own king. Since their own king is a gift from Yahweh they will not be able to appeal to Yahweh to save them from his measures.

Perhaps the most significant element in the reply of the people is their suggestion that a king will 'wage our wars'. The introduction of monarchical rule will make it much less possible to think of Israel's enemies as anything but 'the king's enemies' and of Israel's wars as anything but 'the king's wars'. Times are changing and the likelihood is of the new kings coming between Yahweh and his people. The meeting at Ramah leads indirectly to the dedication of Solomon's temple.

1. *Can christians fight a holy war without self-contradiction?*
2. *Is 'national sovereignty' necessary now for the defence of the worthwhile in the world?*


## C. 1 Sam 9:1–10:16. The coming prince.

The people accept Samuel's assurance that Yahweh will give them a king and go back to their homes to wait on events.

**1 Sam 9:1.** At this point the editor joins another piece of material to his main Samuel narrative. There is a certain clumsiness about the joining since he has to insert parenthetically an explanation as to why Samuel is called a 'seer' in this story and not a 'prophet'.

This new source material has the delightful romantic character of the fairy tale. It tells of the handsome young man who sets out on a quest with only one servant and comes after three days to the house of a wise man where, after he has been greeted by maidens at the well and brought to the house on the hill, in which a meal is ready for him as the chief guest, and slept until dawn, he is given the secret message that he is the prince of the land

and that on his way along the road home he will meet
two men by the tomb, three men going to the shrine, one
carrying three kids, another carrying three loaves, and a
third carrying a wineskin, and then he will be caught up
in the music of wanderers and be 'turned into another
man'. All this comes true.

The tale is at least as beautifully told as the country
folk-sagas of other cultures, and has much in common
with the pilgrimage legends of the *Odyssey* and the *Grail*,
but it is not simply a fairy story or a legend. The narrative is carefully shaped to demonstrate the will of
Yahweh in all the events of the journey.

There is a general movement of proclamation through
the story. Saul is always the man who is known to be
coming. The verb *ragad*, 'to announce' occurs in 9:6, 8,
18, 19; and 10:15, 16 (twice), and is closely connected
with the word used for Saul's new office *nagid*, which
means 'the man who has been announced'. Saul is not a
king as the kings of the heathen were king, he has no
claim to the royal rights, he is simply the man chosen by
Yahweh and announced to the people. The announcement is made by 'the man of God' after the sacrificial
meal celebrated at the shrine, and the prince is anointed
'by the Lord', who himself sends his spirit upon Saul.

Saul now belongs wholly to Yahweh. Though he came
looking for his father's asses, he returns with no nearer
relative than an uncle to greet him because he has
become one of those who have no father or home of their
own (10:12). Saul has come among the prophets.

*1. Does the fairy-tale character of this narrative make it less
convincing to the modern reader than a plain unvarnished tale?*

*2. In what sense can a man be 'set apart' for the service of
God?*

**D. 1 Sam 10:17–11:15. Finding the king**

**1 Sam 10:17.** The previous section shows signs of being
an amalgamation of two accounts. There is here a
totally different tradition of how Saul came to be king of
Israel. The first story is made up of material which
probably originated in Ramah and in Ramathaim-
sophim. This second account seems to belong to the
Mizpah shrine. The editor was no fool. He certainly
must have noticed as quickly as we do that there were
inconsistencies between the two accounts. He must, therefore, have seen reasons for setting them down one after
another.

It may be that the editor saw in this successive placing
of the stories an opportunity to stress the fact that Saul
was first of all the prince announced by Yahweh and only
secondarily the king chosen by the assembly of the
people. Even the mere finding of the designated Saul at
this assembly can be effected only by recourse to Yahweh
by lottery and 'inquiry' of the Lord. When he is brought
from the baggage train Saul is announced by Samuel as
'him whom the Lord has chosen' (10:24). Those who
join him are men 'whose hearts God had touched' (cf
1 Sam 7:3). There is some evidence that the story of the
lottery was originally distinct from the account of Saul's
being acclaimed because he was a fine figure of a man.

**1 Sam 11:1–15.** The siege of Jabesh-Gilead by the
Ammonites is the background to yet a third (or fifth, if
we count separately, as we certainly should, the dual
sources of the first two narratives) explanation of how
Saul came to be king.

We are back to the situation as it was after Aphek. The
townsmen know that they are not likely to be rescued.
Israel is too weak to help them, and the Ammonite

knows it too since he utters a threat and leaves them seven days to escape him.

The messengers evidently tell their tale to a hopeless crowd. The theme here, as in the earlier stories, is of the Israelites' total inadequacy to deal with the huge dangers which confront them. Yahweh rescues them again. He 'leaps' on the young farmer and is so manifestly present that the 'fear of the Lord fell upon the people' and they muster to serve under his command. It is not Saul's military fame (he is only a farmer like the rest of them) which renews their confidence but the evident power of Yahweh which is now in him. This later becomes a significant distinction. The people follow Saul, and he knows they follow him, not for his own personal skill and courage (nor even, here, for his handsome figure), but for the presence of Yahweh in him. Like the rest of them, Saul is nothing without the spirit of Yahweh. After the account of the victory which Saul himself ascribes to Yahweh, the Jabesh narrative ceases and the Gilgal shrine's tradition of the kingship is added on.

The six sources we can now uncover in our present text may have come to the editor already shaped into three, and even if we grant, gratuitously, that he could not see the complexity of the material he was given, he would still have to make his decision to include such apparently repetitious materials. I think that he probably rejoiced in his accumulation of diverse traditions because its very multiplicity demonstrated that a new thing had been brought about in Israel and that no one human explanation could exhaust the meaning of Yahweh's act. The Lord of history had created the kingdom of Israel.

*1. How can we now recognise the leap of the spirit on a man in our society?*

*2. Do we need such an inspired man since we all have a share
in the Spirit through baptism?*

### E. 1 Sam 12:1–25. Samuel retires

**1 Sam 12:1 ff.** Samuel recognises the political dangers
which threaten a man who relinquishes power. He may
be blamed for a convenient negligence or corruption
when the new leader finds the situation too much for him.
He wants to make sure that he is acquitted of any mal-
practice before he is accused. He has the more reason to
want to be assured of this total release from guilt in the
memory of the accusations levelled at his sons (cf 1 Sam
8:3).

Having gained a decree of innocence, Samuel can
move on to allotting blame. The old man reviews the
history of the Hebrews from the time of Jacob, through
the exodus and the settlement in Canaan, up to the
recent Ammonite threat. At every point in this history
the people are described as forgetting Yahweh and
turning to false gods until they come to their proper
senses and come crying to Yahweh for rescue. The
sermon leads up to a description of the people's cry for a
king at the coming of Nahash as yet another example of
the way in which they try any remedy first rather than
trust in Yahweh. The new king is, however, the gift of
Yahweh, he is Saul the *saal*, 'the one asked for' by the
people. Everything depends on the conduct of the
king and his people. If they keep their hearts turned to
Yahweh they will prosper. If not 587 waits at the door.

The historian has therefore, in the manner of Thucy-
dides, given Samuel the right thing to say at the close of
the period of the judges. The events of the past are set out
as an expression of the continuing fidelity of Yahweh in

the face of the continual infidelity of Israel. The events of the future under the kings are hinted at in order that the whole history may be understood as the working of similar forces in the world.

   *1. What would count today as evidence for the faithfulness of God?*

   *2. What would now seem the most helpful institution for God's work in the world?*

# 4
# King Saul
# 1 Sam 13:1–15:35

### A. 1 Sam 13:1–15. The first disaster

The demand among the Israelites for a king originated in
their need to have a permanent leader of a standing army
(1 Sam 8:20). The Philistine threat could only be
answered by the election of a king. From this it followed
that the success or failure of the monarchy could be
gauged by victory or defeat in the field. The king had to
be a warrior. It is natural, therefore, that the first act of
Saul's reign should be the sounding of the battle trumpet.

This was a courageous act for, despite the minor
success of Jonathan against the prefect of a Philistine hill-
fort at Gibeah-Elohim, it was highly unlikely that the
unarmed (1 Sam 13:19) Israelites would manage to
make much of a showing against the military efficiency of
the five towns. It was almost a foolhardy act, for the
Israelites were not anxious to join Saul, who had made
Israel odious to the occupying army, and crept into holes
and crannies as soon as the Philistines roused themselves.

Since the battle was on the plains the Philistine
chariot was an almost unbeatable weapon, and the
scurry of the men of Israel to the hills if not laudable is
understandable. Saul, understandably impatient with
the tardiness of Samuel, himself performs the war-
sacrifice and no sooner has he done so than the old man
appears to say Saul's action is certainly not laudable.

We find it difficult not to sympathise with Saul, and the editor certainly sets out his arguments in a strong brief, but the purpose of the Gilgal narrative is to show that from the beginning Saul relied on himself and such self-justifying arguments, not on the faithfulness of Yahweh. He is committing the great sin against which the whole history is composed. He trusts his own flesh more than the vital spirit of Yahweh. He is unlike Hannah with whom the story begins and too like the kings who continue it. Already, therefore, Yahweh is thinking of a new prince who is now announced. This hint of David sets the hero-king at the beginning of the history of the monarchy as a chosen saviour.

### B. 1 Sam 14:1–52. The rout of the Philistines

**1 Sam 14:1.** The two sides were encamped on the opposite banks of the Wadi Es-Swenit, and the young Jonathan evidently dislikes the long day's wait for a move from the enemy. He takes his squire on a private exploit.

The folly of leaving the general safety of the camp alone and descending into the valley and climbing up to the defences of the Philistines is not minimised in the telling. Quite the contrary, it is said to have been accomplished only by the power of Yahweh who delivers the panicky uncircumcised heathen into the hands of an army of two. 'The Lord saved Israel' (1 Sam 13:23).

At this sign, Saul, who has begun the ritual for discovering the will of Yahweh, tells the priest to take his hand out of the bag without taking up one of the lots; it is now perfectly clear that Yahweh wants the army to pursue the retreating Philistines. In order that the pursuit be fully carried through, Saul makes an oath to Yahweh for the people that no one will stop to eat or drink. He is taking Yahweh's victory as a serious sign of the day's importance for the liberation of Israel.

Jonathan does not hear of the oath and when he is tired out refreshes himself by eating some of the famous wild honey of Canaan. He learns of his father's oath from one of the troops and does not bother much about it, after all he is now strong enough to continue harrying the enemy. Yahweh must be pleased with this for Yahweh has begun the victory.

At the end of the day the hungry warriors slaughter the animals and guzzle down the meat in a totally informal manner. Saul, always careful of the rubrics, is horrified at the way in which the slaughter has been done without proper form and altar.

As evening comes on the king thinks of carrying on the pursuit of the still-running Philistines, but to his dismay Yahweh does not any more encourage his hopes of a great victory. Saul at once concludes that someone in the army, perhaps even himself, has offended the Lord. He sets about discovering the cause of Yahweh's silence. The lottery which designates Jonathan as the culprit and the young man's own admission lead, Saul thinks, inexorably to his being sacrificed to Yahweh. The people will have none of this. Jonathan is for them simply the young hero who has brought about Yahweh's victory. Saul is perplexed. He wants to appease Yahweh for Jonathan's violation of the solemn national oath, and he sees the truth of the national argument that Yahweh is pleased with Jonathan. He adopts the compromise of releasing Jonathan and ceasing the pursuit. He cannot go on.

The narrator has put here a story which brilliantly demonstrates Saul's character. He is seen to be a good man relying on Yahweh to guide him but yet unable to understand what Yahweh wants him to do. The conflict this sets up is certainly the origin of the manic fits of depression which become more frequent as his reign continues.

**1 Sam 14:52.** The round of military activity in which Saul engaged and his constant seeking out of new fighting men to help in the work are significant not only as an account of how Saul tried to avoid his puzzlement by ceaseless occupation, but as an explanation of the arrival of the new prince.

*1. How much should we rely on a sign to make clear God's will for us?*

*2. What kind of sign would convince us?*

*3. Is Jesus sign enough in our world?*

## C. 1 Sam 15:1–35. The second disaster

**1 Sam 15:1.** The holy war is now continued, at Yahweh's express command, against Amalek, the old enemy of Israel. But it is continued as if it were one of the king's wars. The best cattle are kept by the king and the people and the heathen leader is taken back as a prisoner, perhaps with a hope of a large ransom payment.

Confronted with his sin against the holy war of Yahweh, Saul pleads every kind of excuse, such as his intention to sacrifice the animals, and the strength of popular pressure on him to permit the retention of booty. To these Samuel replies with an uncompromising demand for obedience rather than sacrifice, and a reminder that the man anointed by Yahweh is of no little consequence and cannot be bullied by his troops. Saul is at once cast into his periodic gloom and asks that Samuel stand with him before Yahweh. The old man refuses, declaring that Yahweh has removed his favour from the disobedient king. As he turns to go, Saul panics and snatches at the robe of the prophet, pleading with him to stay.

The tearing of the robe becomes a sudden sign, a dramatic picture of the meaning of the event in which Saul and Samuel are involved. The incident is seen by both as a prophetic word from Yahweh. For the historian and his readers there is here another faint trumpet in the distance announcing the coming prince.

Appearances, however, have to be kept up. Samuel goes once more with Saul to the sacrifice and on the way demonstrates the difference between king and prophet. Samuel hacks Agag of Amalek into pieces and then turns sadly away from Saul. Samuel himself is caught in a puzzlement almost as great as that of the pitiable king. The old man knows the will of Yahweh but finds it hard to give up his friendship with the king.

The whole historical narrative leads inexorably to the theological judgement that nothing less is demanded of a king than total fidelity to Yahweh. If this be lacking then there is nothing but an empty show.

# 5
# The prince
# 1 Sam 16:1–31:13

## A. 1 Sam 16:1–20:42. Coming to court

**1 Sam 16:1.** David is now chosen by Yahweh. Samuel, who is evidently known to have quarrelled with Saul (16:4), comes to the house of Jesse to anoint the new man and is warned at the start of the proceedings not to judge, as the mob judges, by looks (cf 1 Sam 10:24), but by the judgement of Yahweh: 'This is he'. Samuel anoints David within the circle of men assembled before Yahweh for the sacrificial ritual. As in the story of Saul's anointing, the whole emphasis is placed upon the choice of Yahweh and the coming of his spirit: men do not make kings in Israel.

**1 Sam 16:14.** The contrast of David and Saul is made at once, with the declaration of Saul who once was leapt upon by the spirit of God being visited by an evil spirit. The work of Yahweh in history is plainly visible in the servant's suggestion that David, who has until this moment kept sheep on his father's farm, be brought to the centre of public action.

**1 Sam 17:1.** The success of David with the lyre, the favour he finds with Saul, the promise of the king's daughter as his bride, and the military glory he wins by the contest with Goliath and the chase of the Philistines

back to Gath and Ekron, are equally signs of the spirit of
Yahweh working for the young man.

The fact that there are obvious difficulties in recon-
ciling the several narratives of David's coming to Saul's
court is evidence that versions of such an important event
sprang up at various places, just as they did when Saul
was the chosen man. When Yahweh elects a new man
everyone talks about him.

**1 Sam 18:1.** The friendship of Jonathan and David is a
particularly attractive witness to the winning character of
the new man, and of his being brought by Yahweh into
the very midst of the royal house.

**1 Sam 18:6.** The favour of Yahweh on David is evident
to all. Saul begins to recognise him as the man who will
supplant him, the men make him a popular hero and the
princess falls in love with him. By this favour David
comes, despite the king's mistrust, to occupy a more and
more important place in the nation's affairs.

**1 Sam 18:20.** The suspicion Saul has of David leads him
to use Michal as a bait to place David in the dangerous
thick of the fight. Yahweh works through this. The
device recoils. David is successful and marries the princess.
He is now seen to be very much a possible legitimate
successor to Saul.

**1 Sam 19:1.** Saul then openly announces that he will
have David killed. Jonathan, having warned David to
hide awhile, is able to convince the king that to take the
life of a man so obviously innocent and so equally
obviously blessed by Yahweh would be a capital sin. An
uneasy courtesy is restored.

**1 Sam 19:8.** This is broken in one of Saul's dangerous

fits and David has to be hurried away in the night. The narrator emphasises that as the king's son had once done the work of Yahweh so now the king's daughter is the divine instrument. Saul, rejected by Yahweh, has no call on human aid even in his own family.

**1 Sam 19:18.** Saul's attempt to wrest David from the sanctuary of Samuel at Naioth brings him into full conflict with the holy. He is thrown naked on the earth.

**1 Sam 20:1.** Like the princess and the prophet, the prince now helps David against the king. The historian thinks it very important that David should not seem to be chased away like a renegade or a bandit. He must be given the most respectable support from abandoning the court otherwise men might wonder whether he really belonged there at all and whether the whole notion of his being destined for the kingship was not a mistake. Jonathan's parting words are royal evidence of the will of Yahweh.

*1. What do we understand by 'an evil spirit'?*

*2. What does it mean to say that a man can be rejected by God?*

## B. 1 Sam 21:1–31:13. The fugitive

**1 Sam 21:1.** In 19:18 ff, the historian is concerned to show that David had the support of the prophetic element in Israelite society. In this chapter he produces evidence that the priests helped on his career. All those who were in any way representatives of the Lord in the nation are shewn approving David's leaving the court and actively assisting him against Saul. The prophets and the priests, that is, are described as recognising that the Lord is now with David and no longer with Saul. Any suspicion, therefore, of David's actions being treacherous and unholy is dispelled.

The association of David with these two groups, later represented by his two friends Zadok the priest and Nathan the prophet, is both a support for his claims and, once he is enthroned, a claim on him to favour these groups.

The lies told by David and the involvement of innocent men in his rebellion are recounted without either blame or praise. They are certainly not thought to take him out of the sphere of the holy; he and his men eat the bread of the priests and he is given the sword from the shrine. David becomes the perfect knight; there is an Arthurian quality in this situation of deception and holiness inextricably together in the one champion.

**1 Sam 21:7.** The reference to Doeg is a careful hint of the malice which waits outside the shrine. It may be that Doeg is not a shepherd from the hills but rather an important royal official who represented Saul's cultic interests. Certainly at some shrines the flocks who provided the raw material of the sacrifice were very large and had lots of herdsmen to look after them, over whom stood the highest secular official of the shrine.

**1 Sam 21:10.** David moves into Philistine territory and almost gets himself killed or imprisoned. He survives by feigning madness.

The story is difficult to integrate with the other escape narratives. It is awkward to suppose that he would have gone with the sword of Goliath straight to the long-memoried Philistines (cf 1 Sam 29:4 ff where the same song is recalled) and asked for asylum. Perhaps the historian could not abandon this piece of tradition, even though he did not know quite where it belonged in the general narrative, because it so clearly announced in one short passage that David is 'king of this land', and that his degradation is so complete (he lets his spittle run down his beard) that his effective rule can only be brought about by the power of Yahweh.

**1 Sam 21:13.** David pretends to be mad in order that Achish will not believe his servants and in order that their primitive awe of madmen will prevent the Philistines from attacking the stranger.

The text is obscure. It may be that the Masoretic text is to be preferred to the Septuagint text in this verse and that David 'scribbled on the doorposts'—modern men often put their names and professions on their doors, good Jews set prayers, and ancient Egyptians put both names and prayers on the doorposts of their homes and, more elaborately, on the entrances of their tombs, for example the six stelae of Puyemre's façade. Perhaps David defaces Achish' gateway prayers to his gods. This might seem a particularly dangerous thing to do, but the very wildness of the act might well itself be a convincing demonstration of the madness of the doer.

**1 Sam 22:5.** The need to rely totally on Yahweh is emphasised by the succeeding narrative of the prophet Gad's advice. David is told not to run off to alien towns but to stay within the holy land of Judah under the protection of Yahweh.

**1 Sam 22:6.** The protection of Yahweh is, however, a complex matter. The next incidents show that Yahweh's participation in history does not prevent men working against him. The sinister Doeg becomes the instrument of Saul's revenge on the priests at Nob. This sacrilegious act commits Saul to a policy against the Lord. The historian

wants his readers to realise that there can be no friendship with Yahweh in a man who hunts the Lord's
anointed. To be at enmity with David is to be at enmity
with the prophet Gad and the priest Abiathar.

**1 Sam 23:9.** On David's being warned that the men of
Keilah will ungratefully surrender him to his enemy,
Saul continues the man-hunt against all odds. Yahweh
hides his servant. Jonathan accepts David as the coming
king. The mountains rise between pursued and pursuer.
The very Philistines divert him from the attack. Small
wonder that Saul has doubts of his own success.

**1 Sam 24:3.** In the next section the cave opens its mouth
to deliver Saul into David's power but the perfect knight
sees in this a temptation to violate the sanctity of the
anointing and snatch by force what must be received as a
gift from Yahweh. It is difficult to fault the wisdom of the
advice David's men give him; they have been hunted up
and down and their enemy has a superior force. To kill
him there and then would be completely to reverse
advantages. It is difficult to appreciate David's sense of
the inviolable sacredness of the man who no longer has
Yahweh with him. The historian, at any rate, thought of
his action as neither foolish nor generous but simply a
proper acknowledgement of the holy character of the
king of Israel. Certainly practical advantages derive from
David's honouring the anointing even in Saul from whom
the Lord has departed. If he had killed Saul and become
king, he would have set a dangerous precedent in the
manner of swapping rulers. And as it turns out his action
leads to a further proclamation of his royal destiny: from
Saul himself!

**1 Sam 25:1.** That David is not always so aware of his

responsibilities before Yahweh is brought out in the story of the 'fool' Nabal and David's quick rush to put him and his men to death. This headlong fury is halted on the hill path by Nabal's wife Abigail, who is evidently understood by the historian as a messenger of Yahweh. She prevents David (attributing the prevention to Yahweh, however, 25:26) from the sin he resisted in the cave. He gives up his intention to take matters into his own hand and become involved in blood guilt. Immediately after this Abigail, like a prophetess, speaks of the sure house David will receive from Yahweh (cf 2 Sam 7) because he is the prince of the holy war.

The death of Nabal is a conclusive sign in this story of the Lord's purpose being worked out for David.

**1 Sam 26:1.** The second story of David sparing Saul re-asserts the meaning of the first, but coming after the story of Nabal, it shows what is going to happen. Saul admits that he is like Nabal (26:21) and has been a fool, and the reader knows at once that a violent death is being prepared for him.

**1 Sam 27:1.** The historian has made great efforts to balance the assurances that Yahweh is with David by descriptions of the hunted life he is forced to lead. At the moment when we understand for certain that Saul's quick death is coming, David is shewn to be so afraid of the king that he enlists as a feudal dependant of the Philistine commander of Gath. The call of David across the valley to Saul was mainly concerned to put the blame for his leaving the land of Yahweh and taking service with the foreigner squarely on Saul (1 Sam 26:18 ff). The historian is most anxious that this, the most am-biguous act of David's life, should not be used by his opponents to prove that David was ever less than wholehearted in his care for Israel. He therefore makes it plain that David deceived the Philistines and took Ziglag from them pretending to raid the villages of their enemies whilst actually destroying the enemies of Israel. The fief of Ziglag is David's first possession and forms the nucleus from which he makes his empire.

**1 Sam 28:5.** David is in exile playing a very dangerous game among his enemies but it is Saul who knows himself to be at the end of his hopes. He has killed the priests, the prophet gives him no comfort. The witch has conjured a spirit which can only remind him of the moment (which he must have re-lived so often in his misery) when Yahweh went from him.

**1 Sam 29:1.** Immediately we are told of David being confronted with the worst crisis of his career. It would seem that nothing can now save him. Either he has to go to war against Israel and thus forfeit at once his character as the coming prince of his people, or he has to refuse and be, like Coriolanus, cut down by his employers. David's dilemma is set in parallel with that of Saul in the previous chapter. Neither can rescue himself. Saul is told plainly that Yahweh is not with him, he is to die in the next battle. David is rescued by Yahweh in quite unexpected manner. The Philistines refuse to take him along with them to the battle line. He does not have to refuse their command nor fight against his people. He can go home to Ziglag, leaving the Philistines and Saul to fight it out.

**1 Sam 30:1.** The reader breathes a sigh of relief and is suddenly jolted into anxiety. The historian's purpose in chapter 30 is to demonstrate that David's kingship was always a gift of Yahweh. At no moment in his career could David rest assured that glory was just around the next rock. His destiny was certain but it was not to be worked out by man's political devising.

**1 Sam 31:1.** Not even the death of Saul and his three warrior sons (described by the historian with noble sympathy) clears the way for David to be king of all Israel. Not every man of his people had lost admiration for their anointed king and would want the outlaw to rule over him (the men of Jabesh-gilead for example, took great risks to serve their dead champion). Nor was he the only choice. Saul's commander Abner put forward Ishbaal the surviving son of Saul as the next ruler. The very Philistine victory which took off Saul put much of the Jordan area in their hands, making it impossible for the Israelites there to choose any king at all.

*1. Is there any lesson for us in the 'Robin Hood' episodes of David narrative?*

*2. Do we live as if God would rescue us from danger? Would it be a good thing if we did?*

# 6
# David the king
# 2 Sam 1:1—9:13

## A. 2 Sam 1:1–5:5. Mounting the thrones

**2 Sam 1:1.** The reverence David felt for the anointed man, which had restrained him when Saul was in his power, is now expressed in his fury with the Amalekite. Though the man seems to have lived peaceably among the Israelites and to have been with them in the battle it is significant that it should be a man of this hated stock who dares to kill the anointed king of Israel. He is cut down.

The killing of the Amalekite is a sign of David's real distress at the death of Saul. The lament confirms this impression. If no other of the songs attributed to David were really his, this lament would be explanation enough of his reputation as a great bard.

**2 Sam 1:18.** *The book of the Upright* seems to have been a collection of songs, cf Josh 10:13, 1 Kgs 8:53. The lament of David must be primitive. It is for 'the sons of Judah' and must have been composed before David had been accepted king of Israel.

**2 Sam 2:1.** David now takes his wives and moves out of Philistia back into Judah. If he is to have a chance of being king it will only be as a man of the land. Hebron was the site of a shrine set up by Abraham and a central meeting place of neighbouring tribes.

76

Though not all the men of Judah are David's friends (cf 1 Sam 23:19; 26:1), it seems taken for granted among them that David is to be their new king.

**2 Sam 2:5.** David's total assurance that he is the proper successor of Saul is demonstrated in his commendatory letter to the men of Jabesh-gilead. A service done for Saul is a service done for Saul's inheritor. The loyalty of the men of Jabesh-gilead is assumed to have passed quite naturally to the man who is now anointed.

**2 Sam 2:8.** Abner, the cousin of Saul, evidently wishes to be kingmaker in Israel. *Ishbosheth* means 'man of shame'; he is also called (1 Chron 8:33, 9:39), *Ishbaal* or 'man of Baal', and it seems likely that these are both anti-Saul changes made by the editors in the original name *Ishvi* or 'man of Yahweh' (cf 1 Sam 14:49).

**2 Sam 2:12.** The games at the pool suddenly became serious. Men died. A battle took place. Joab and his brothers, cousins of David, pursue Abner. Abner hopes to avoid killing Asahel because this will involve him in a blood-feud with Joab. He stops running too suddenly for Asahel to stop himself crashing onto the butt of Abner's spear. He falls on the blunt shaft and is there transfixed.

The hunt continued until Abner made a stand on a hill-top and the two armies retired homeward through the night. This is the beginning of the civil war which finally set up David as king of the two nations.

**2 Sam 3:6.** While David is shewn to be increasingly the established man (hence the list of his sons 3:2–5), his rival's party begins to disintegrate. Abner throws his weight about. He takes for himself the concubine of Saul (a significant assertion of lordship, this, as Ishbosheth remarks; cf the stories of Absalom, 2 Sam 16:22 and

Adonijah, 1 Kgs 2:13), and quarrels with Ishbosheth so
thoroughly that he is prepared to betray his kingling to
David. All this is seen by the chronicler to be the working
of Yahweh's will for David. Even Abner knows that
David is chosen by Yahweh (3:9).

**2 Sam 3:13.** David demands Michal back as evidence
that he is legitimately successor to Saul. It is remarkable
that Ishbosheth allows Michal to be returned and that he
does not oppose Abner visiting David. His conduct is so
unsuspecting as to be stupid.

**2 Sam 3:20.** Abner assures himself of the inclinations of
the influential men of Israel and goes to parley with
David. Abner goes from Hebron 'in peace'. This sounds
as if some pact had been arranged between the king and
the general. Certainly Joab and his men think it significant that Abner goes 'in peace'.

It is significant too, that David does not defend Abner
in reply to Joab's accusations. Joab takes his silence as
permission to use his own judgement in the matter. Joab
seems to have suspected that David would make Abner
commander-in-chief as a reward for his part in the king-
making business. He acts quickly. He avenges Asahel and
secures his own military command.

**2 Sam 3:26.** David realises that people will suspect that
he lured Abner, the only strong man with Ishbosheth,
into his camp to have him murdered. His anger against
Joab is an expression of the ruin of his political plans and
his fast a public demonstration meant to reach Israel that
he is the innocent victim of Zeruiah's family feuds.

From the beginning of his reign David's court was an
arena of factious fights. The next incident illustrates
what such fights could come to.

**2 Sam 4:1.** David realises, as he did when the Amalekite brought the news of Saul's death, that his own security is involved in the maintenance of law. He has Ishbosheth's murderers killed. The editor establishes (4:4) that there is no other member of the dead king's family who could be a possible rival to David.

**2 Sam 5:1.** David is now elected king of Israel by the northern leaders who come as petitioners to Hebron and then the elders come to anoint him. If the subsequent history of the monarch is to be intelligible, it must always be held in mind that David was now ruler of *two kingdoms* united only in his person.

## The anointed king

The accounts of Samuel's formal appointment of Saul and David as Yahweh's kings in Israel make it plain that from the beginning the kings of Israel were anointed with oil. Why this ceremony? It was not, after all, common among near-eastern courts and temples to anoint the new kings. The only society of note to use this ceremonial was the Egyptian. And in Egypt the man anointed was the minister or military vassal of the Pharaoh on his appointment to some office in the two kingdoms.

It may well be that, at least by the time of David, the anointing of the king was understood in Israel as the appointment of the man to an office under Yahweh. The king of Israel was a vassal of Yahweh. This would give particular significance to the man as anointed and would therefore account for David's veneration of Saul as the anointed man of Yahweh, (1 Sam 24:6, 26:9; 2 Sam 1:16). The vassal of Yahweh would be protected by Yahweh.

David's view of the anointing as recruitment to the household of Yahweh may have been strengthened during his stay in Hebron, for the kings of this town had certainly at one time been vassals of the Egyptian Pharaoh.

*1. Is David too much a* politician *to be a* hero *today?*
*2. Does the anointing of a king or a priest mean much in our society?*

## B. 2 Sam 5:6–6:23. Setting up the capital

**2 Sam 5:6.** David's possessions have no central focus. Ziglag, Judah, and Israel need to be brought into one structure. This cannot be achieved by David's living in either Judah or Israel for the men of the other kingdom would fancy themselves slighted. David needs a new city which will belong to him personally and not be an embarrassing gift from either. He needs a city which has no historical connections with any tribe. He needs a geographically central city from which he can control all possessions. He decides on Jerusalem.

The men of this old Jebusite hill-stronghold think their defences so impregnable that blind and lame men could garrison it against attack. Their assurance is another indication of the desirability of the fortress town. No man could capture Jerusalem unless Yahweh were with him (5:10).

**2 Sam 5:11.** The mention of the king of Tyre emphasises the increasingly important position David has in Levantine politics.

**2 Sam 5:13.** This position at home is rendered the more secure by a series of marriages and the establishment of a wider complex of family loyalties.

The Philistines had no reason to attack before David's accession to the throne of Israel, since until then the Israelites had been contained in two weak kingdoms. The king of both kingdoms who ruled from the central fortress constituted a real threat to Philistine influence in the area. The Philistines try to outflank David and divide Israel and Judah by coming down to the plain of Rephaim.

David's total reliance on Yahweh is brought out both by the references to Yahweh giving the Philistines into David's hands at Baal-perazim and at the second encounter, and by the note that the pagan idols were left abandoned on the field.

**2 Sam 6:1.** The defeat of the Philistines gave David time to demonstrate to his peoples his enjoyment of Yahweh's favour. He decided to bring the ark, the old sign of Yahweh's presence with his confederate people, into his city. This would manifest Yahweh's approval of the new king and show him to be the inheritor of the covenant promise.

The ark had been at Kiriath-jearim just the Israelite side of the border from Philistia, and had therefore been under the supervision of the enemy. David's defeat of the Philistine made it possible to bring the ark into the centre of his political complex.

The accident at the threshing floor seems to David particularly bitter for it suggests that Yahweh does not approve of the move to Jerusalem. It appears very odd indeed to us that God should strike a man who was trying to help him. The explanation of the narrative may possibly be in the belief that God, like some atomic reactor, is so powerful that unless he is treated circumspectly, whether Yahweh wills it or no, a careless man is likely to be overpowered, or it may be a ritual elaboration of this fear. Perhaps the editor intends his readers to understand how necessary it is, even for the priests, to observe the cultic rules before approaching the divine presence.

**2 Sam 6:12.** At any rate the next incident shows that Yahweh's presence is manifest in fruitfulness and prosperity.

The king resumes his dancing procession, the proper sacrifices are offered and the feast begins as the ark is placed in the tent prepared by David.

**2 Sam 6:16.** Michal looks out of the window. At once the Israelite reader would understand that she was not accepting the duty of a true worshipper of Yahweh. The proper thing was to join with the king and the servant-girls in the feast of Yahweh. Her refusal to take part in the round-dance before the ark is both the sign of her apostasy and the final cause of the rejection of Saul's family.

David points out that he is aware of the proper human responses to Yahweh's presence and that because he has served Yahweh he has been put in Saul's place. The editor points out that Michal's irresponsibility before Yahweh leads to a situation in which no grandchild of Saul can succeed to the throne.

The significance of this section of the narrative is twofold. It establishes David as the proper custodian of Yahweh's ark, and therefore the inheritor of the promise to the nation, and it lays stress on the barren flesh of his wife so that the reader is left wondering (despite the two lists of commoner-sons) how a royal successor will be born to carry on the promise after David's death.

The story, that is, both suggests that David is to be the

first of many kings and makes it difficult for the reader to understand how this should be.


## A note on 2 Sam 6:16

Many commentators have shewn that in ancient Egypt royal audiences were often given from a window or balcony, and probably this custom is referred to in Gen 26:8 where Abimelech, the Philistine king, looks from his window and sees Isaac and summons him to his presence. This narrative is a parallel to the Egyptian sequence of Gen 12:10 ff and the king at the window incident may be a relic of the source material. At any rate, the reference to the Philistine is an evident anachronism in the patriarchal narrative, showing that some details have been changed in the telling.

It may be that a formality similar to that of the Egyptian rulers characterises Michal's watching of the entry of the ark into Jerusalem. Michal is, as it were, observing the proceedings from the royal box. If this is the case she is adopting an inappropriate foreign custom. She ought, obviously, to have been with the serving-women at the festival, sharing in the popular rejoicing like her husband. She is told as much when he returns. The speech of David (6:21–2) is not simply a raking over the past with an unpleasant reference to his in-laws; the king is teaching his wife what the servant-girls understand, that the only appropriate attitude before Yahweh is one of humble gratitude. Michal has not the first instincts of a true Israelite.

I think that the editor of this piece of the David-tradition means us to realise the foreign, and indeed pagan, outlook of Michal from his first mention of her. There are two, or perhaps three, other occasions in the old testa-

ment when women are described as looking out of their
window:

**1. Jgs 5:28.** The queen-mother waits at Harosheth for
news of her son Sisera's victory against the army of Barak.
She looks out of her window (same verb as in the Michal
story) for the charioteer who will bring the good news.
But the enemy of Yahweh will not return, the heathen
Philistines have been defeated. The pagan queen has
misplaced her confidence.

**2. 2 Kgs 9:30.** Jezebel painted her eyes and looked out of
the window of the palace at Jezreel. She intends perhaps
to undermine Jehu's stern purposes, but she gets her
deserts and is thrown down to feed the dogs. Since she
had been the royal protector of the Baal-Herakles cult
(cf 18:4, 18:19, 19:2) her murder is a triumphant sign
of the end of the ascendancy of Tyrian paganism.

**3. Prov 7:6.** This is the doubtful case. The Hebrew
represents the narrator as looking out of a window. The
Greek suggests that the woman is on the watch for her
victim but this does not easily agree with verses 10–12 for
there the woman is already in the street. Even if this is
the true reading, the woman who looks out is certainly
up to no good and is well placed in a category which
includes the painted Jezebel.

The editor of 2 Samuel certainly knew the traditional
accounts of Sisera's mother and Jezebel; he may not have
expected many of his readers to have recognised the
allusion in his narrative but some may have been alerted
to it by his opening description of the queen. To these, the
story would have seemed an exposition of a character
already known by this vignette. Michal at the coming of
the ark to Jerusalem has already placed herself among

condemned idolaters when she appears at the window.

## C. 2 Sam 7:1–7:29. Two houses

**2 Sam 7:1.** The peace which followed the Rephaim victories over the Philistines and which enabled David to arrange the bringing of the ark to his city was long enough for the king to consider other matters. Probably the 'rest' after victories during which the events of this chapter occurred was that after chapter 8 or chapter 12. David is not yet secure enough for such business as chapter 7. The historian places the events here because they follow well upon the ark story.

Having built himself a house, David suggested to Nathan, the senior religious adviser of his court (Abiathar is already taking a back seat) that a temple be built for the ark of Yahweh.

Nathan thought this not to be at all in Yahweh's interests. We may be puzzled by his opposition and by the editor's belief that such an opposition could be inspired by Yahweh. The more impressive the shrine of the ark the more honoured would be Yahweh, we might suppose. Nathan and his supporters have other considerations in mind. The ark is the sign of Yahweh's covenant with the people. The ark is their protection against every coercive power. To Nathan it seems that by bringing the ark into his own private territory David is signifying his intention to channel the promise of Yahweh through himself. David is attempting to be a mediator between Yahweh and his people. The ark will gradually come to be acknowledged as the sign of the promise to the royal house.

If the king builds a temple to house the ark then the

sacred sign will be effectively controlled like any other royal possession in the treasury and the freedom of the people be in jeopardy.

So Nathan appeals to the exodus tradition when the ark was associated with the people and their camp and no one had even thought of kings. He refuses to countenance David's building a royal house for Yahweh.

**2 Sam 7:11.** At the same time Nathan promises that Yahweh will make a royal house for David.

This material has been written and re-written several times. It would seem that a primary affirmation that Yahweh is not a local god who must keep in one place (not even Shiloh or Jerusalem) has been overlaid first with a promise to the whole people and then with a promise to David. This last promise, (7:11, 12a and 16), has been elaborated in order that 'Solomon in all his glory' shall be acknowledged as the king promised by Yahweh.

**2 Sam 7:18.** David's prayer begins, as does every formal expression of what it means to be a Hebrew, with an account of the past care Yahweh had for his people which leads up to the present manifestation of his providence.

The prayer is the second part of the promise-response structure of the divine giving of the message and the king's acknowledgement of the message. The accounts of both parts are constructed by the historian so that the reader will realise the unity of David and the people of Israel before Yahweh, and the everlasting character of this unity.

It ought also to be kept in mind that David in the prayer repeatedly (7:19, 20, 21, 25, 26, 27 twice, 28, 29 twice) refers to himself as the *servant* of Yahweh. The servant-character of David's position becomes of great importance later in the narrative.

## The king chosen by God

The great promise of the royal covenant (2 Sam 7) is not simply a narrowing of the covenant with Abraham (Gen 15) but an Israelite expression of a common notion in near-eastern monarchies. The king is king because he is chosen by God. Eannatum, the early dynastic ruler of Lagash speaks of himself as 'called to mind by Enlil'; Hammurabi describes himself as 'the chosen shepherd of Shamash'; Shalmaneser III of Assyria attributes his throne to the wonder that 'the great lord Assur, in the steadfastness of his heart, singled me out by his dazzling gaze'.

David's obscure origin makes it all the more evident that he must be the chosen king of Yahweh, he could not else have risen to so great a height. His shepherd boyhood is all in his favour. Assurbanirpal II was less fortunate; his father Shamsi-Adad IV was king of Assyria before him. He ruled only by mere hereditary right. His official proclamations hide this uncomfortable fact. He says to the goddess Ishtar, who must have known all this to be a pious fraud, and in the hearing of his courtiers, who must have smiled at so innocent a piece of propaganda, and his people, who saw the necessity of such an election:

> Thou didst take me from among the mountains;
> Thou didst call me to be a shepherd of men;
> Thou didst grant me the sceptre of justice.

It thus appears that the pastoral traditions of David were remembered not so much for romantic pleasure as for political expediency. The pressures of general near-eastern prejudice and of particular Israelite belief both made it desirable that the king should be able to attribute his rule to divine choice rather than human blood and cunning.

*1. Is the messianic expectation of the editor, and of later Hebrews, different from modern hopes of a time when we shall be able to affirm 'we've never had it so good'?*

*2. Must a nation conquer others in order to respect itself?*

*3. Can we appreciate today the way in which a particular political settlement was thought to be the will of God?*

*4. Is there a divine right of democracy any more than a divine right of monarchy?*

## D. 2 Sam 8:1–8:18. Davidic imperialism abroad and at home

**2 Sam 8:1.** The chronicler suggests a link between David being promised a 'house' and his success against the Philistines. 'After this' he never looked back.

**2 Sam 8:2.** The old Moabite power remembered in the tale of Ehud and King Eglon (Jgs 3:12 ff) had been friendly to David (cf 1 Sam 22:3), but had evidently proved untrustworthy. Some enormity must have been committed to merit the fierce enaction of two out of three prisoners being executed. Moab becomes a tributary power and may have been absorbed into the central Davidic system.

**2 Sam 8:3.** David's defeat of Hadadezer who ruled an Aramean state north of Damascus shows that his power extended as far as 'the river' Euphrates.

Hadadezer's allies come from territory neighbouring on David's kingdoms and therefore like Moab they are

brought within his direct jurisdiction and forced to pay
tribute.

**2 Sam 8:9.** Others realise the presence of a new power in
the Levant and send ambassadors and gifts to ally themselves with David.

**2 Sam 8:12.** The chronicler adds the names of those old
enemies, the Ammonites and the Amalekites, to his list of
conquests and the conquest of the men of Edom and the
garrisoning of their land tacked on to make the list of
victories more impressive.

David has now ringed his kingdoms round with
tributary states, timorous allies and defeated enemies. All
this is said by the chronicler to be the gift of Yahweh
(8:6, 14). It is certainly difficult on any other explanation
to account for the astounding success of David and his
establishing Israel and Judah as a major force in the
Levant. Certainly the traditional limits to Israelite
growth did not obtain during this period: neither Egypt
nor Mesopotamia were ready to interfere with David's
ambitions at this moment. But it is still wonderful that
the energetic king of such a small state could accomplish
so much abroad.

**2 Sam 8:15.** At home the civil service multiplied and
ministerial officials with separate jurisdiction were recognised at the court.

Justice, however, was administered by the king himself. As the empire became larger and more mercantile
and the old order creaked from the new pressures the
number of cases before the royal court increased vastly.
This led to a great back-log of litigation and the king,
who never gave up his personal presidency of the court,
was much blamed for the hardship that the delays pro-

duced. The slow processes of law were a main grumble at the time of Absalom's *coup d'état* (2 Sam 15:2 f).

The beginnings of later court intrigues are present in the command of Joab over the army and of Benaiah over the foreign bodyguard of the king, and in the uneasy alignment of the two priests, Zadok keeper of the ark and Abiathar the Aaronic priest who had shared outlawry with the king.

The chronicler has put together two notable indications of the growing imperial power of David, widening boundaries and growing bureaucracy. But he has put them together not to emphasise the personal marvel of David but to demonstrate how effective is the promise of Yahweh. Events reveal a continuing providence which works towards the future everlasting reign of the house of David. Political developments are indications of divine activity, history is the material of theology. David, from the time of his anointing by Samuel, through his outlawry and the anxious time of his election by the kingdoms, has been led by Yahweh to this imperial splendour. His success is a guarantee of the coming messianic kingdom.

*1. What are the advantages and disadvantages of having a special sacred building in a community?*

*2. Is Hebrew nationalism any more respectable than British or American imperialism?*

### E. 2 Sam 9:1–13. The last remnants of Saul

If the history is to show David legitimately succeeding to the kingdoms and his family legitimately established as the rulers of the people of Yahweh, all relics of Saul must be accounted for and tidied away.

Some clearing of the decks has been done already:

(a) Jonathan, Abinadab and Malchishua, the sons of Saul, were killed with their father at Mount Gilboa, 1 Sam 31:2.

(b) Abner, who is a relative of Saul, was murdered by Joab, 2 Sam 3:27.

(c) Ishbosheth, Saul's remaining son, was assassinated by the two captains, 2 Sam 4:7.

(d) Somewhere along the line the two sons of Saul and Rizpah, and the five sons of Morab, Saul's daughter, were ritually murdered at the fertility ceremonies of Mazzoth at the sanctuary of Gibeon, 2 Sam 21:1–14.

David consented to this and was accused by Shimei, a distant relative of Saul, of having murdered these unfortunates himself. 2 Sam 16:7 f.

(e) Michal, Saul's daughter, is barren, 2 Sam 6:23.

**2 Sam 9:1.** David now asks if any member of Saul's family survives. There is only one, Meribbaal, the crippled son of Jonathan. David brings this man into his court. Certainly Jonathan's son is given a place of honour in the palace, but he is also safely under David's supervision, now no plotter could use him against David.

The danger from Meribbaal is emphasised by the reference (9:12) to his having a son.

*1. What is the value of an hereditary succession to power?*

*2. Is it surprising that, at a time when so sophisticated a piece of writing as this history is being created, men would indulge in fertility magic and ritual murder?*

# 7

# The end of the affair
# 2 Sam 10:1—24:25

## A. 2 Sam 10:1–20:26. The succession story

(1) **2 Sam 10:1.** *The Ammonite war* may well be that of chapter 8. It is used here as a setting for the Bathsheba story.

(2) **2 Sam 11:1.** *Bathsheba.* The king looks down from his summer house on the flat-roof of the palace into the courtyard of a neighbouring house. He sees Bathsheba, the wife of one of his own mercenaries. He commands her presence.

This is a dangerous time for both of them; the adulteress and the adulterer are both within the law. Bathsheba says she is going to have a child. Uriah, her husband, has been away on too long a campaign for anyone to believe that the baby is his, and anyway the town must have known what was going on.

The king begins to extricate himself with the simple device of recalling Uriah from the front and sending him home to his wife. The device does not work.

David gets Uriah drunk. Still he does not lie with his wife.

The royal power is then brought into operation. Uriah is deliberately set in the thick of the battle and left to die at the gate of Rabbah. Other men died also.

Bathsheba goes through the outward shows of mourning, marries David and bears a son.

**2 Sam 12:1.** The parable of Nathan brings home to David the terrible injustice of his treatment of Uriah.

The figure of Nathan produces some difficulties for the reader. It is a puzzle to determine his status. Was he a prophet who had, because of his powers as seer (cf Samuel) and his manifest holiness, free access to the king? Or was he the king's tutor?

Texts in the archives of Man, a city state on the middle stretches of the Euphrates, dating from the time of Hammurabi (that is, c 1700 BC or 700 years before the Davidic period) speak of a *muhhum* or ecstatic prophet who brought to the king's council messages from the god Dagan. These messages came in dreams and were taken as political directories. There is at least one Man text which represents the god as having put the king on the throne and having the right to remove him if the divine will is not obeyed.

Nathan may be a man of parallel authority for parallel reasons. The Uriah incident may not have been the first time he interfered in David's conduct of affairs.

Certainly the prophetic men of Israel's history thought it part of their proper concern to indicate Yahweh's political will. The narratives of King Ahab and the 'son of the prophet' (1 Kgs 20) and the same king's meeting with Elijah after Naboth's murder (1 Kgs 21) or of Jehu, the son of Hanani, announcing the impending ruin of Baasha (1 Kgs 16) show the same pattern of prophetic activity, and the Ahab incidents have the 'Thou art the man' element of personal denunciation. Once Samuel, the seer and prophet, had been instrumental in making first Saul and then David king in

Israel, the genuine prophetic element in Israelite public
life had no fear of asserting the superior authority of
'Yahweh who reigns'.

Nathan himself is described as a king-maker in the
struggle for the succession during the last days of David's
reign. His influence, combined with that of Bathsheba
and Zadok, was just strong enough to defeat the candi-
dacy of Adonijah, the nominee of most of the councillors,
and to secure the designation of Solomon. There is no
suggestion in the narrative that Nathan was either unused
to speaking with the king or that he was shy of con-
fronting David with a harsh reality. The servants of the
king are later depicted as afraid to tell him of the child's
death, and their predecessors in Saul's court must have
often wished themselves elsewhere. Nathan shows no
anxiety for himself.

The form of Nathan's announcement is taken from the
herald-form of contemporary Levantine custom. The
near-eastern messenger was trained to present his information in a way which make his own understanding
and interpretation of the message quite unimportant.
The herald would introduce his verbatim report of the
royal message with some such formula as 'Thus spoke the
king: I have considered . . .'. The death sentence Nathan
conveys to David has this character; it is totally the word
of Yahweh.

At the same time Nathan does understand the message
to be conditional even though the form is not. He can
remit the penalty. He has some area of negotiation even
though he is not Yahweh's plenipotentiary.

It is noteworthy that the king at once accepts the
blame and does not storm against Nathan. The narrator
does not wholly alienate the reader from the king even in
this story. Nor does he suggest that Yahweh has finished

with David. Though Nathan condemns the king to death there is one way to save himself. David is not too vicious to miss it. The king repents and is pardoned.

Punishment remains. In the future a man will take David's wives from him as he stole Uriah's wife. In the present the child of sin shall die.

The realist accepts the child's death. It may be that the child is understood by David as a sacrifice for sin and its death a sign that Yahweh accepts the sacrifice. This would explain why he wears the penitent's sackcloth during the illness and doffs it when the child dies.

There may be a resonance here of the popular notion that Yahweh, like Moloch, demands the sacrifice of the first-born. Abraham made a similar mistake and was shewn that Yahweh wanted service, not human sacrifice.

**2 Sam 12:24.** There is certainly a resonance here of the biblical theme of the second son inheriting the blessing of Yahweh. The Abel story and the Jacob story are examples of this. Christ is later said to be the 'second Adam'.

But the narrator does not want to make too much of the birth of the second son of Bathsheba; he intends the reader to hold this information at the very back of his mind while the problem of David's successor is rehearsed in the next chapters.

(3) **2 Sam 12:26.** *The Ammonite war again.* The conclusion of the war redounds to David's credit and increases his economic power. The narrator has thus brought his readers back to the normative position from which they may have strayed during the previous story. David is the favoured king. He is the king who received Yahweh's promise.

Again the question arises: 'Who is to succeed David

and carry on the promise?' Even if the answer comes immediately, 'Solomon', the reader may yet be intrigued by the question, 'How can Solomon succeed when David has so many elder sons?'

To this question the rest of the book and the first chapter of 1 Kings are addressed.

(4) **2 Sam 13:1.** *Tamar:* David's sexual passion is repeated in his son.

The crown prince Amnon lusts after his half-sister Tamar. He cannot see how to get her since a young virgin of her high rank would be carefully protected. The suggestion of his cousin Jonadab that he pretend to be ill and ask for the princess as his nurse is adroit. The king will do anything for one of his sons, particularly for the heir; he orders Tamar to cook a tasty dish for Amnon.

The girl comes to the prince's suite, prepares the food and, in order to please the sick man, herself brings the food to his bedside. Amnon leaps at her, forces her onto the bed and rapes her. When he has done he is filled with revulsion for the girl and despite her pleadings has her turned out as a common prostitute. The description of the princess in her torn dress, weeping as she went to her brother, is beautifully done.

Absalom cannot comfort her. She knows as well as he that her life is ruined. No man will marry her now. She knows too as well as he that David dotes too much on Amnon to punish her ravisher.

David is angry but incapable of dealing with his son. He forgives. Absalom is angry but incapable of dealing with his half-brother—yet. He waits.

(5) **2 Sam 13:23.** *The sheep-shearing.* Amnon behaved as wantonly as David had with Bathsheba. Two years later Absalom behaves as brutally as David had with Uriah.

Absalom invites the court to a sheep-shearing party and in the course of the meal his farm-workers hack Amnon to pieces, perhaps with pitch-forks and scythes.

The banquet breaks up in such confusion that the first reports are that all the sons of David have been murdered. The princes mount their mules (the royal beast) and ride pell-mell to Jerusalem. Absalom flees the country and takes refuge with his grandfather. David's personal grief at the death of his heir is augmented by the public loss of the next in line. The house seems doomed to fail.

**(6) 2 Sam 14:1.** *The wise woman of Tekoa.* The realism that characterised David's attitude to the death of Bathsheba's first child comes to the fore again in this story. Three years are long enough for him to think about a reconciliation with Absalom.

Joab puts the woman of Tekoa up to her trick and though David guesses at once what is going on he seems glad enough of the opportunity to recall his handsome son to the capital.

He cannot, however, yet bear to see the murderer of Amnon. Absalom, whose sons must have died young (cf 2 Sam 18:18), is not only a handsome young man, he is a determined, ambitious prince. The story of Amnon shows that he can be really dangerous. His burning of Joab's fields demands attention and receives it. He commands the situation. Joab reconciles him to the king. David kisses him.

The narrator does not comment on David's actions but the bare facts are enough for the reader to be aware of the recurring flaw in the king's character. He cannot deal with his family affairs. He has not control over his emotions. Skilful though he is in political intrigue and military tactics he is unable to cope with his lusts and his favoritisms. Any reader would wonder after this story what audit Absalom must make of a king who kept him five years from the palace and then hugged him. To a man like Absalom who had kept his mind on Amnon's death for two years David must have seemed a strange weak thing.

**(7) 2 Sam 15:1.** *The civil war.* Absalom set about dethroning his father with considerable skill. He exploited the backlog of cases in the royal law court by hinting to the petitioners that if he had the handling of affairs their business would move speedily to a successful conclusion. He was prepared to buy golden opinions from anyone who could be charmed by a smile or a bow—that is, from almost every man.

**2 Sam 15:7.** At the end of four years Absalom judged that he had enough ministerial and popular support to bring about a successful *coup d'état*.

He receives permission from David to leave Jerusalem to go to Hebron. This city is chosen because at the religious festival of the ancient shrine many men may gather without arousing suspicion.

Absalom's choice of Hebron is a hint that he will work for a restoration of 'the good old days' before the king became crotchety and difficult. In the first days of David's reign the court resided there. David had won the support of the men of Hebron by presents of booty from his raiding parties (1 Sam 30:26–31) and, after the death of Saul at Mount Gilboa had set up his home there and been anointed king 'over the house of Judah' (2 Sam 2:4). It was likely, therefore, that this shrine, which had lost prestige by the removal of the court to Jerusalem and the installation of the ark, would be a centre of discontent and that those who came to the shrine for the local festival would at that very time be more than ever aware of the difference between the shrine's golden age of the first years of David's reign before the murder of Ishbosheth and the meagre present. The prince's arrival for the festival would of itself suggest that here was a chance to make Hebron a force in the land and therefore a chance for a better way of life. Absalom offered the pilgrims a political weapon. They rallied.

The conspiracy is given a new probability of success by the arrival of Ahithophel, the experienced counsellor, who seems to have been retired from David's council in Jerusalem since he is at his farm in Giloh when Absalom's message arrives. He may have real power over the prince. Or he may simply have known what Absalom was planning and have made some pretext to go to his farm so as to leave Jerusalem unhindered. At any rate he is the brains of the revolution.

**2 Sam 15:14.** On hearing the news, David is at once certain that he cannot resist the popular pressure for Absalom. This is surprising. David takes it for granted that he cannot count on Judah and Israel is already lost. He knows he has lost his people's love.

The king takes his family, his body-guard, the foreign legion, and the newly arrived Philistine troops of Ittai, out of the city.

David leaves the priests with the ark in Jerusalem. This is the first sign of his new appeal to Yahweh. He accepts his misery as the will of the Lord and hopes that his ready acceptance will be rewarded by a change of fortune.

David is now seen by the historian as the true servant of Yahweh walking in penitence along the pilgrim way.

The king crosses the dried-up bed of the Kidron and walks up the Mount of Olives to the summit shrine.

At the same time his refusal to carry the ark with him not only allows every choice to Yahweh (cf Hophni and Phineas who tried to force Yahweh to defeat their enemies), but is a careful stroke of policy: David has his informers in the capital.

**2 Sam 15:32.** At the shrine David has news of Ahithophel's joining the conspirators against him. He turns to Yahweh for help.

He is greeted by the councillor Hushai who wants to go with the king into exile but who will be a burden on the journey and a useful fifth column in the council of Absalom. He is sent back to be another member of the resistance with the priests and their sons.

This passage combines, like the previous one, a dutiful sense of everything being in the hands of Yahweh, with a careful use of every opportunity for human ingenuity and effort.

**2 Sam 16:1.** Ziba's tale is credible since we have already been told of David's anxiety to deal with any possible pretender from Saul's family, and Meribaal is the only one left to grab the kingdom.

David might be the more likely to believe Ziba because of his memory of Ishbosheth trying to hold the kingdom while Abner and David quarrelled. A weak man always waits for the flight of the strong.

The king may also have wondered for a moment whether he had so offended Yahweh that the kingdom was being given back to Saul's family. His uneasy conscience makes him unable to deal ruthlessly with Shimei.

But the picture of the patient king, slowly plodding along the valley path pelted with clods of earth and abused by a ruffian in front of his men, makes the reader pause. It may be that David's sins are great but he seems now a noble figure. Yahweh cannot throw him over.

**2 Sam 16:14.** The king comes to Jordan and is refreshed.

**(8) 2 Sam 16:15.** *The rebel's success.* Absalom enters Jerusalem in triumph and at the moment of success commits a fatal error of judgement. He accepts Hushai as an adviser.

**2 Sam 16:22.** On the advice of Ahithophel the prince goes in to his father's concubines in full view of the people. This is a significant act because:

(*a*) Absalom is asserting his entry into all the royal dignities and privileges.
(*b*) Ahithophel has made sure that there can never be a reconciliation of the king and his son. Such a reconciliation was obviously possible in view of David's doting favouritism for his sons, and it would have left Ahithophel unprotected against the king's revenge.
(*c*) Nathan's prophecy has come to event. What David did to Uriah has been done to him in return.
(*d*) Absalom has brought a curse on himself and has lost the rights of the heir (cf Gen 35:22; 49:37).

The question yet remains how so many of the Israelites could be content to allow the anointed king to be turned off by a rebel. It looks at first sight as if they cared nothing at all for the will of Yahweh expressed in the choice of David in Saul's place.

In fact they do care. They act in precise obedience to the precedents. Yahweh's will is not a magic but a continuing relationship. It is precisely because the Spirit of Yahweh left Saul and came on David that the men of

Israel are prepared to believe that the Spirit has gone from David.

Yahweh's kings have come to their thrones through their election by the people. Absalom has been elected. There is a good case, therefore, for saying that Absalom is king. Everybody recognises this. David himself when warning Ittai to serve Absalom recognises the possibility: 'Go back and stay with the king' (2 Sam 15:19). Hushai makes this thesis the explanation of his change of allegiance, 'Him whom the Lord and this people and all the men of Israel have chosen will I serve' (2 Sam 16:18). Absalom himself certainly believes that he is truly king. His actions are those of a king. He goes in to the royal concubines.

**2 Sam 17:1.** But since Yahweh has not gone from David, Absalom is not truly king of the people, and therefore his very exercise of the royal prerogatives brings down a condemnation from Yahweh. At the moment of exaltation, before all the people, he ruins himself. This chronicler had no need of lessons from the Greek tragedians.

Absalom should, once he had stepped in so far, have followed Ahithophel's advice and pursued David at once. But Absalom is a doomed man. Hushai persuades him to a foolish course. David is given time to get across the Jordan and organise his troops for a guerrilla war at which he is past master. David's prayer at the Mount of Olives has been heard, the wisdom of Ahithophel has been turned aside.

**2 Sam 17:15.** The spy network of David gets the message through.

**2 Sam 17:23.** Ahithophel is now convinced that Absalom's rebellion will fail and though it is likely that the prince will be pardoned the men who counselled him will be horribly murdered. He rides his aristocratic mount home to Giloh, tidies his desk, makes his will and hangs himself. The depth of his despair is measured by the fact that he is one of the only five men in the old testament who are recorded as having committed suicide, and of the other four one was dying of a woman's blow and wanted to save his honour and two belong to the much later period of the Maccabees.

It is the final blow to this great councillor that we do not know his real name. *Ahithophel* means 'my brother is folly', and is evidently the name that David's party gave him after the rejection of his advice and the success of David's prayer that his wisdom might be turned to folly. His long career went for nothing. The scribes consistently call him by the nickname which commemorates his final failure.

## David the servant

For christian readers the story of David's exile and Ahithophel's suicide has strange resonances.

David leaving the city with his few friends, crossing the brook Kidron, praying on the Mount of Olives and bearing with patience the abuse of his enemies as he walks the road to shame is a shadow of Jesus, like the shadow that moves ahead of a man when he walks with his back to the sun.

Ahithophel the traitor, advising the enemies of David and finally hanging himself in a tree, is a shadow of Judas.

The likenesses become both more complicated and more revealing if the patient misery of the king who is so often called 'the servant of Yahweh' is recognised as the original of the sufferings of the servant figure in Deutero-

Isaiah. It may well be that when David at last returned to Jerusalem that he himself understood that it was through his acceptance of suffering that he had come to his throne. He may himself have made up songs on this theme, or others may have sung ballads at the camp fire and hearth. Such songs may be both the beginnings of the literary form of the suffering servant songs (Is 42:1–4, 49:1–6, 50:4–9, 52:13–53:12) and the shapers of their themes. If this is the case then there would be a strong connection between the sufferings of David at this period of his life and the passion of Christ. There is little doubt that Jesus' self-understanding was in part shaped by his knowledge of the suffering servant songs.

If there were such suffering servant songs about David's exile and restoration it may be that they were not preserved in the official archives because Solomon did not care to be reminded of the civil war episode. For a people to remember that David was turned out of Jerusalem might encourage malcontents (of whom there were many in Israel during Solomon's reign) to chance another uprising. The tradition of such servant songs would then have been maintained only in the country villages, forming a lively popular tradition unconnected with the official courtly tradition.

The royal tradition maintained a different account of David. Paying little attention to the disgraceful episode of Uriah and the disturbing facts of David's inability to govern his own family, the scribes made of David an heroic ideal and set this ideal as a standard for all succeeding kings. In the history Solomon (1 Kgs 3:3) Asa (1 Kgs 15:11) Amaziah (2 Kgs 14:3) Ahaz (2 Kgs 16:2) Hezekiah (2 Kgs 17:3) and Josiah (2 Kgs 22:2), are all measured against the legendary David who becomes 'the king'. The royal history is seen as the

history of David and the successive kings are judged good
and bad so far as they fit the davidic pattern. The coming
kingdom of glory will be a time when David's crown
'bursts into flower' (Ps 132:18) and the Spirit of Yahweh
rests on 'a shoot from the stock of Jesse' (Is 11:1).

**(9) 2 Sam 17:25.** *Absalom, my son.* Absalom knows the
military prowess of Joab's family. He puts Joab's cousin
in charge of his army and crosses the Jordan in pursuit of
the king.

**2 Sam 17:27.** David is now seen by some men to have a
good chance of defeating his inexperienced son. His
stores are replenished, his men increase in number, and
the battle-field suits his peculiar genius.

Absalom might have won in a pitched fight along the
battle-lines but he has no idea of how to conduct
skirmishes and sallies among the trees. He is not good
with trees at all. His mule runs on while Absalom is held
fast by the neck in a fork of a terebinth.

Everyone knows that David cannot hate this enemy
(18:5 f) and no ordinary soldier dare take the responsibility of killing him (18:12) but Joab sticks the young
man like a pig and his bodyguards thrust their spears in
the swinging body. Telling David is more difficult than
killing Absalom.

The king breaks down and his sobs are heard throughout the camp. Only Joab has sense and insensitivity
enough to jostle the king into thanking his troops for the
victory. If this had been left undone hardly any of them
could have been relied upon to come if the trumpet
sounded another day.

**(10) 2 Sam 19:9.** *The return journey.* Everything is now re-
versed.

(*a*) The men of Israel who had rallied to Absalom now

decide for David and claim the right to be his bodyguard back to Jerusalem. If he allows this David will be their nominee. He appeals to Judah to redress the balance and show an equal welcome.

(*b*) Joab who has killed the enemy leader loses command of the army to Amasa the defeated general.

(*c*) Shimei comes out to greet the man at whom he had throwns the clods of mud. He is the first man of Israel to welcome David and must have been pretty sure that the king could not start more squabbles that day.

(*d*) The arrival of Ziba and Merribaal threatens to make for unpleasantness on the day of rejoicing and David has no time for their quarrels.

(**11**) **2 Sam 20:1.** *Sheba*. Absalom's main support had come from the men of the ten tribes of Israel and these northerners were never quite content to be ruled from Jerusalem. Sheba appeals to a popular sentiment (which will on Solomon's death divide the kingdom) and rallies roughly the same forces as Absalom had attracted at Hebron.

The cry 'To your tents, O Israel', is the signal for the end of the campaign and reminder that the old exodus tradition of a free people had only been put aside for a few years (since the election of Saul) and might well be taken up again.

**2 Sam 20:4.** The situation requires quick action if Sheba is not to be a threat equal to that of Absalom or greater, and Amasa's tardiness constitutes a real danger. He himself probably realises this because he hurries to Gibeon and arrives there before the force under Abishai. Joab's career has been stopped by Amasa's promotion and the murder leaves him again (as did the earlier murder of Abner) the only possible commander in chief.

**2 Sam 20:13.** Once the body has been disposed of even the troops of Judah who had begun their march under Amasa's command accept Joab as their general. Abishai retires from the supreme command in favour of the experienced and dangerous general.

**2 Sam 20:15.** Joab does not have to make a fight of it. He realises that any further show of force against Israel will antagonise the tribes even more. David's security depends on Israelite contentment. Sheba is a pawn in the bargaining.

There is some parallel between this incident and that of the recall of Absalom. In both a wise woman, full of traditional lore and modern instances, cooperates with Joab to settle a dispute which threatens David's throne.

**2 Sam 20:22.** Joab returns and is confirmed in his command. David may not care for the murderer but he cannot do without him.

The succession story has come, however, to another dead end. Every member of Saul's family has been killed or contained by David, Amnon the crown prince has been murdered, Absalom the next heir has been killed in a civil war.

Who remains to be king in Jerusalem after David? Who is to inherit the promise of Yahweh?

*1. Is the death of the baby acceptable to modern readers as a divine punishment of David?*

*2. What concept of providence dominates the succession story? Can a modern reader be content with this concept?*

*3. Does David remain a hero for the reader of this narrative?*

## B. 2 Sam 21:15–24:25. Yahweh reigns

The stories which follow the settlement of the Absalom

and Sheba wars are meant to bring to the fore the reality of Yahweh's providence. The narrator may have supposed his story to have concentrated for a while a little lop-sidedly on the human alarums and excursions. The next sections make it quite clear that nothing could be done in Israel without the good will of Yahweh. The narrator adopts stylistic devices here which have proved useful before in putting across the idea of divine action among men.

(1) **2 Sam 21:15.** *The giants are destroyed.* This is a story told in the folk-lore manner of the choosing of Saul or the exploits of the shepherd-boy David. Giant after giant is lopped down by David's men. That David is old and unable to defend himself is a detail akin to the plight of the wounded king of *Parsifal* or the last days of Arthur.

It has been suggested by more than one commentator that the slaying of the giants shows us David's triumphant defeat of the last giants of pre-history. Like Jack in the fairy-tale he opens the way for a world in which man is the steward of God.

The narrator's point in telling the story of the giants is to emphasise that the events of human history are not explicable in human terms. The strangeness of the giants who could only be defeated by more-than-human power leads the reader to the recognition of divine activity in all the events of David's career. He has been the coming prince, the daring outlaw, the suffering exile, and (despite his also being the lustful king) he has been the returning hero before whom all enemies among men and giants are rolled back by Yahweh.

(2) **2 Sam 22:1.** *The song of thanksgiving.* The king himself recognises that Yahweh has been saving him through his history. He may well be the author of this psalm, (it is

number 18 in the psalm collection), since he can hardly have been given the reputation of a psalm-singer without some foundation in fact.

The psalm is a theology of Davidic history. The power of Yahweh has been exercised to protect David from every enemy but that power has seemed even to him a fire and a whirlwind. The psalm touches on several incidents in David's career:

(*a*) *2 Sam 22:21.* The story of David is replete with moments when other men recognise that he is the chosen servant of Yahweh but none more effective than when Abigail comes to him with a warning to keep his hands clean of the blood of the fool Nabal. Her stopping him in the man-hunt left Nabal to the fury of Yahweh.

(*b*) *2 Sam 22:28.* However much David may have abused his power as king (notably in the affair with Bathsheba) he continually recalled to mind that he was only king at all because Yahweh had removed his Spirit from Saul and had taken David from the sheep-fold to be the king of his promise.

This was brought out in the account of the welcoming of the ark into Jerusalem when Michal despised him for dancing in the streets. Their quarrel was fundamentally a quarrel about how a man should hold himself before Yahweh. David knew then that Yahweh exalts the lowly and puts down the mighty from their seat.

(*c*) *2 Sam 22:44.* The results of the wars with Philistines and Moabites, and the Aramean campaign (cf 8:1–8), was that 'David won a name for himself' and the king of Hamath sent him tributary gifts of friendship.

(*d*) *2 Sam 22:49.* The 'men of violence' who set out to kill David are probably the leaders of the various rebel-

lions in the northern kingdom. The psalm seems to com-
memorate David's rescue from enemies at home and
abroad.

(*e*) *2 Sam 22:51*. The climactic favour of Yahweh is of
course the promise elaborated in Nathan's prophecy.
This promise gave a future and a destiny towards which
all other events tended in the davidic history.

This promise is an expression of the 'steadfast love' of
God, the *hesed Yahweh* or *hesed 'elōhīm* that was to be
celebrated so wonderfully by Hosea. This divine love
creates trust and sympathy and peace among men. David
himself shares this love with other men. The Lord stands
'between' David and Jonathan (1 Sam 20:42) and to
Jonathan's son, Meribbaal, David shows 'the kindness of
God', *hesed 'elōhīm* (2 Sam 9:3).

(**3**) **2 Sam 23:1.** *David's testament.* Like Moses, David
follows his canticle with a word for the future.

The distinctive feature of the future is the destiny of the
dynasty. From the time of Moses onwards the leaders of
the tribes have always been called by the Spirit of
Yahweh to perform a particular service for his people.
The Spirit came on Gideon (Jgs 6:34) and he rallied the
people against the Midianites, and after the victory
Gideon retired. The Spirit came on Jephthah (Jgs 11:29)
he defeated the Ammonites and retired to Mizpah in
Gilead. The Spirit seized Samson in the vineyards of
Timnah (Jgs 14:6) he killed the lion and went on his way.
So even with Saul. The account of the Jabesh-Gilead
campaign is cast in the same pattern. Saul is called by
Yahweh to rescue his people, 'the Spirit of Yahweh
seized on Saul' (1 Sam 11:6) and this operation reveals to
the men of Israel that Saul is the chosen man to get them
out of their present difficulties. But the Spirit goes from

Saul (1 Sam 16:14). The gift of the Spirit of Yahweh to
David might have seemed to his contemporaries to be
similarly a one-generation if not a one-emergency affair.
The difference between David and all his predecessors as
leaders of Israel is the 'everlasting covenant' Yahweh has
made with him and his heirs.

The testament of David, like the previous two sections,
is designed to place the total responsibility for the glory
of the davidic line on the favour of Yahweh.

(4) **2 Sam 23:8.** *The warriors of the holy war.* It is noticeable
that though the prowess of the soldiers is explicitly
recorded, their victories are ascribed to Yahweh's power
(23:10,12). No human endeavour can achieve its purpose without divine aid.

**2 Sam 23:13.** David is certainly pictured in the incident
of the cup of water as a man who is hero-worshipped by
his men, but he is also pictured as a man and not to be
worshipped. The soldiers risked their lives for him, they
offer him water at this price. David does not dare accept.
Life can only be offered to Yahweh. The 'three' are therefore almost personifications of the holy war; their exploit
belongs to Yahweh. Whatever other men do they are not
numbered with 'the three' (23:19, 23 and probably end
of 24), and indeed it looks as if the chronicler has set
these three in apposition to the murderous three, Joab,
Abishai and Asahel.

Lest the reader be swept away in enthusiasm for the
hero David, the last name in the list of his warriors brings
him back to reality and the remembrance that no man is
a total hero.

(5) **2 Sam 24:1.** *The census.* The wickedness of the census
is twofold. David's plan to number the people will give

him a bureaucratic dictatorship and allow him to manipulate men as if they were objects. Our present dislike of identity card and passport numbers is in accord with this objection.

More importantly for the historian the decision David takes will enable him to raise a royal army and disband the tribal levy which has up till now fought Yahweh's wars.

David acknowledges his guilt before Yahweh but is still aware of reality enough to choose Yahweh as his executioner in preference to man (24:16 shows the soundness of his judgement).

The vision of the angel leads to the final witness of Yahweh's favour to the davidic line in Jerusalem. The temple of Yahweh is to be built in the midst of David's city.

*1. How are we to distinguish between proper governmental control and bureaucratic snooping?*

*2. Is any aspect of human life fundamentally private?*

## C. Unfinished business

The narrative of 1 and 2 Samuel ends with a splendid announcement of Yahweh's everlasting covenant of presence. In one sense, therefore, the narrative is a shapely story of the way in which the worship at the shrine of Shiloh is legitimately connected with the worship in the temple of Jerusalem. Not the final section only but the whole narrative is the *hieros logos* of the Jerusalem shrine.

But in another sense 1 and 2 Samuel is incomplete and unsatisfactory as an historical narrative. The story of the succession which has occupied so large a part of the whole history is left in mid-air. The explanation of this curious circumstance is to be found in the estimate the historian had of Solomon. The succession story seems to us a David-story and ought to be cleared up in the David-narrative, but to the historian Solomon was the great king, greater than David, and therefore the last part of the succession story is thought of as the prologue to the Solomon-narrative and hence it is placed at the beginning of 1 Kings. And that, as Sheherazade might say, is a story for another time.

# 1 and 2 Kings

# 1
# The last days of David
# 1 Kgs 1:1–2:12

**1 Kgs 1:1–4.** There seems here to be an echo of the
primitive notion that the fertility of the fields is linked to
the virility of the king. It may be that the courtiers were
quite unaware of the primitive motives behind their
work to get the king to lie with a new concubine, or it
may be that they had noted the contemporary Egyptian
emphasis on the relationship of the ruler as the living
Horus to the growing of the crops, and that they had in
this as in so much else accepted the Egyptian court as
exemplar for their own. Or the courtiers may have been
simply sympathetic or even cynical onlookers at the
failing of the king's general powers symbolised in his lack
of sexual desire.

It does seem significant, however, that only when the
king has failed to respond to Abishag is he brought to
declaring his son co-regent. The girl came from a village
noted in the *Song of Songs* for the beauty of its women.

**1 Kgs 1:5–10.** Adonijah is evidently Absalom's brother
in handsomeness and luxury. Horses and chariots were
employed by the Assyrian aristocracy but both were quite
uncommon in Israel's civic life. Even in war cavalry was
not much used until after the battle of Qarqar in 853.

It may be that the professional soldiers distrusted the

feudal horsemen and therefore allied themselves for the coming power struggle with the later and more energetic members of the Council led by Nathan and Zadok.

Adonijah, though the eldest surviving son of David, would not in the still newly established monarchy count on an undisputed succession to the kingship. David was less like a dynastic ruler than a charismatic judge, like those of the old heroic period who came into prominence at a particular crisis and whose sons had no expectation of leadership by inheritance. David certainly was making every effort to turn himself into a dynastic ruler but there might be, at the handing over of the leadership at his death, a reactionary call for the people to live again in the old ways of the judges.

The meal was a sacrament of trust and if Solomon, Nathan or Benaiah had been invited Adonijah would have been prevented by the religious and courtly code from proceeding against them later.

**1 Kgs 1:11–40.** The telling of some parts of the story more than once, here and in the narratives of Solomon's anointing and of Adonijah receiving the news of his being outwitted, is a common feature of Ras Shamra texts, and is perhaps here related to the more general features of folk tale and ballad narratives.

We can see in this story of court intrigue the change which has taken place in Israel from the time when Saul was found among the baggage. The whole tone of the narrative is one of political sophistication and small-country factions. Solomon's tutor, Nathan, and his mother hoped perhaps to have a deal of power during the first years of the young prince's reign. There is no evidence other than the ambitious word of Nathan and Bethsheba that David had promised the crown to

Solomon. The story simply shows that Nathan knew well
how to exploit the common ferocity of the senile at the
prospect of another succeeding to authority.

The ritual of anointing is performed at the Spring of
Gihon perhaps because of its associations with earlier
fertility rites (cf Ezek 47 and Joel 3:18). From the
incident of the hurried coronation we can deduce something of the ordinary rites performed at the installation
of a king in Jerusalem. The essentials, which could not be
omitted, are evidently an anointing and washing of the
king, and the presentation of the new monarch to the
people with his royal insignia—in this case Solomon is recognised as king, or rather as co-regent since David has not
given up his royalty, by his riding upon the royal mule.

The ceremony thus proceeds from a recognition of the
king by Yahweh to his presentation for acknowledgement
by the people. The king is divinely authorised before
popularly acclaimed.

**1 Kgs 1:41–53.** This section is beautifully composed from
the moment when the guests steal hurriedly away from
the fallen favourite to the careful subjunctive of Solomon's
promise.

Adonijah having been over-reached thinks, quite
rightly, that Solomon is as capable as he is himself in the
disposal of political enemies. He seizes hold on the 'horns
of the altar' and thus makes himself a part of the sacred
stone of sacrifice. The Jerusalem sanctuary was never so
crowded with criminals as others discovered by Tiberius
in the Near East, but the practice was accepted in
society of the runaway obtaining sanctuary at the shrine.

**1 Kgs 2:1–12.** David had not been so careful in the
phrasing of his oaths so he can only clear old scores by the
hand of his successor. Perhaps it is a grim reality of

politics that the historian recounts when he tells of the dying David instructing Solomon to accomplish the deaths of Joab and Shimei. Or perhaps Solomon and his advisers simply invented the story in order to justify their murderous proceedings and to reassure the rest of the court that no further purges would take place among the old administrators.

The presence of the sons of Barzillai at Solomon's table may have had some political significance since they would be hostages for the good behaviour of the Israelites in Transjordan (cf 2 Sam 9:11–13).

A point to be noted in all the discussions of who is to succeed David is that everyone seems to take it for granted that the successor is to be one of David's sons. This is very surprising. The assumption must have been strange to most of the community for they had never yet lived in a society ruled by a dynastic king. And yet it had to be made. David's political astuteness had made it impossible for any other thought of succession to be entertained. He had brought unity and interdependence to a number of disparate political entities as his personal dependencies. The effectiveness of the new state was bound up with the davidic family. If men wished to belong to a power of any influence in the Levant then they had to accept the realities of politics and continue the federation centred on David.

*1. Are we right to be so wary as we are of relating political and economic events to the will of God for us?*

*2. Should politicians be expected to preserve in their public acts the standards we expect others to accept in private morality?*

*3. Is there, in fact, a private morality any more since we are now so involved in every event? How do we set the limits to what we will take into account when we make a particular decision?*

# 2

# Solomon and the temple
# 1 Kgs 2:13–11:43

**1 Kgs 2:13-46. Solomon secures his throne**

**1 Kgs 2:13-15.** It would be pleasant to think here of a romance between the beautiful village girl and the prince, and perhaps the old lady Bathsheba saw just that. But such an explanation is unlikely to be adequate to the realities of the situation as Adonijah conceived it.

David had taken over Saul's concubines, and Absalom had taken David's harem for himself in his revolt against the king, because the possession of the previous king's ladies was the outward sign of full succession to royalty. Adonijah evidently has not given up the notion of rallying his powerful friends for a palace *coup* and thinks that his having David's last concubine for himself would lend credit to his claims. Solomon appreciates Adonijah's thought and has the young man put to death.

**1 Kgs 2:26-35.** With Adonijah dead his faction lost any hope of protection from the vengeance of Solomon. The high places at court are redistributed. Abiathar ceases to be royal chaplain and Zadok has his appointment in reward for the help he gave during the succession crisis. Joab, being rather more dangerous, is not retired but put to death. The seriousness of Solomon's determination to free himself of the old leaders is to be measured by his willingness to have Joab cut down in the sanctuary. The contrast here with Solomon's earlier respect for 'the horns of the altar' as a refuge may be an indication of his growing confidence in his hold upon the nation.

**1 Kgs 2:36–46.** Solomon waits three years for a chance to put Shimei to death with some show of legality. It is observed that Shimei was told not to cross the Kidron and that he did not do so when he went south. The Philistines seem to have been somewhat like the Bourbons in their capacity not to learn any lesson from their history. Their experience with David should have warned them against employing runaway Israelites.

The use of Benaiah for the killings of Adonijah, Joab and Shimei would suggest that the soldiery had gradually become a royal bodyguard and ceased to think of themselves as local musters. There is growing up a professional military group attached to the king and engaged in a career army. The old system of recruiting the farm-workers for a local campaign is not suited to the new conditions of the organised state.

*1. What part should we now allow heredity in the selection of a ruler? Are sheikdoms demonstrably worse forms of government than presidencies?*

*2. Should we expect the scriptures to offer any guidance on such political matters?*

## 1 Kgs 3:1–5:6. Solomon in all his glory

**1 Kgs 3:1.** The dynastic alliance made by this marriage was with the weak xxi dynasty and had greater religious significance in Israel than political.

**1 Kgs 3:2–3.** Solomon evidently took part in fertility

rituals at the high places—those open-air sanctuaries associated with hill-tops and small groves of trees which the deuteronomist regarded with especial abhorrence.

**1 Kgs 3:4-15.** The divine charism of the judges, of Saul and of David, had given these earlier leaders a title to authority in Israel which Solomon, succeeding by hereditary and political power, did not have.

The Egyptian notion of a king was of one who came out of a divine incubation and acceded as the new Horus, the divine son whose earthly father had been simply a guardian of his youth.

The popular Israelite notions of a charismatic leader and the foreign ideas brought perhaps by the Egyptian queen came together as a demand for some divine authorisation and legitimisation of Solomon as 'the child of Yahweh'.

**1 Kgs 3:16-28.** The story told here is a familiar incident in folk tale and ritual—twenty-two versions have been discovered in various near-eastern texts—and it is attached to Solomon here as an example of his sagacity.

The version recounted here fits well with the character of the king as it has already been demonstrated in the killings of his political opponents. The man who could have Adonijah and Joab chopped to bits would be unlikely to care if a baby got sliced.

The story has Hebraic rather than Egyptian associations for it shows the king as immediately accessible to his subjects (cf 2 Sam 14).

This section is completed at 5:19-14 where the wisdom of Solomon is placed in the category of the practical sense of the Arab sheikh, and is shewn to have been diversified by an appreciation of Arab riddle games (cf 1 Kgs 10:1, and the example in Jgs 14), and an acquain-

tance with Egyptian scribal proverbs, as well as a sophisticated humanist interest in nature which may have
supplied matter for fables like those of Jotham (Jgs 9).

The importance of this wisdom is evidenced in the
practical business of delicate negotiations with such
cunning persons as Hiram of Tyre and the merchant
princess of Sheba.

**1 Kgs 4:1–19.** The list of Solomon's government officers,
which includes ecclesiastics, archivists, army officers,
fiscal prefects and a minister of forced labour, should be
compared and contrasted with the unordered references
to Saul's generals (1 Sam 14:50), the chief of his shepherd and his armour-bearer (1 Sam 31:4) and his
servants (1 Sam 22:6), and with the list of David's
officials (2 Sam 8:15 and 20:23–26).

It should also be remarked that two elements of this
governmental system are totally without precedent in
Israel's history. The corvee had perhaps been used
before by the Hebrew overseers of foreign prisoners but it
seems that only with the accession of Solomon was the
instrument of forced labour employed with Hebrew
conscripts. This constituted a real affront to free Israelites
and became a great grievance to the people. Adoniram
was the first victim of the revolution in the first days after
Solomon's death (1 Kgs 12:18). Secondly, the fiscal
prefects are in charge of areas which are not coterminous
with the old tribal boundaries.

Professor Alt has shewn that some of the Salomonic
districts were centred on the old Canaanite city-states,
but his examination of the districts persuades him that the
new system was simply designed for fiscal efficiency and
was not a measure to weaken the political independence
of the tribes.

**1 Kgs 5:7-8.** It may even be that the division of the territory was simply an arrangement to provide a monthly supply of royal provender and fodder for the horses at Megiddo, and that the districts were decided upon according to their cornbearing capacity.

**1 Kgs 4:20–5:6.** The picture given here of a happy and prosperous establishment all the days of the great king ought to be balanced by thoughts of the successful revolt of Rezan of Damascus and that of Hadad of Edom, and the insurrection of Jeroboam. These were symptoms of general discontent with the policies of Solomon and the means adopted to achieve his political and economic ends.

*1. What makes a political leader worthy of our admiration?*

*2. Is the 'great man' so removed from our littleness that he is beyond our judgement?*

*3. Is each man, perhaps, beyond our human judgement since we know so little about one another?*

## 1 Kgs 5:15–9:26. The temple

This section seems, from stylistic similarities with royal documents in the old testament and at Amarna, to have been based upon the Jerusalem archives. With the exception of the reference to David and his plan to build a temple, which seems to have been part of the later deuteronomic elaboration of the David legend, the material for this section was, therefore, derived from contemporary accounts, perhaps the 'Acts of Solomon' kept as the official annals of the reign.

Tyre, a Phoenician merchant settlement cut in two by four stades of water, was at this time the most obvious growing power in the Levant and was soon to take over the nearby Sidon and a great area of southern Phoenicia.

Solomon and Hiram recognised the advantages of co-operation. Their two kingdoms were not great powers but both were aware of themselves as energetic and developing principalities. Hiram's cedar monopoly and the expert craftsmen of his court workshops made him a most desirable ally for a king with ambitions to be a builder. Solomon's control of the trade routes through Palestine from the Mesopotamian, Arabian and Egyptian manufacturing and marketing districts, and his agricultural surplus of grain and oils made him useful to the Tyrian importer.

The accession of Solomon provided the kings with an opportunity to exchange formal greetings which might be developed into trade talks. If the bargaining collapsed the formal embassy might withdraw without loss of face.

An indication of the priestly character of the writer is his far greater interest in the temple and its furniture than in secular government buildings such as the royal palace about which he seems to have collected very little information or else to have excluded most of his source material from the final version of his history. The writer was certainly not a builder or an architect for even when writing of the building of the temple he often gets technical terms wrong and he relies on rough outline descriptions of some intricate matters of structure. It is thus not possible to reconstruct with any accuracy the details of the temple.

The temple was evidently smaller than the house of the forest of Lebanon (7:2), but it would be unwise to conclude from this that the royal influence overawed all cultic events. Even the frequency of royal interferences in the ritual and finances of the temple should not be taken as demonstrating that the temple was merely a royal chapel. This would be to accept too modern a view of the king himself, for it would suggest that he could be properly thought of as a private person. But in Israel at this time the king was more than a private person, he was the representative of the whole people, and all his official acts belonged to the whole community. Royal influence was national influence.

**1 Kgs 6:11-14.** The deuteronomist has inserted here a theological note intended to keep the reader from supposing that there was some inviolable stability connected with the monarchy. Everything depends for its stability on man's participation in the divine plan of things.

**1 Kgs 6:23 ff.** *The cherubim.* This and other passages in this section of the book have been reworked, perhaps more than once, to include material of interest to priestly editors. The cherubim are described in Gen 3:24 and Ezek, 28 as guardians of paradise, and here they may be guardians of the ark of the covenant and perhaps also of the temple treasury like the Assyrian winged bulls at the gates of palaces and temples. But more probably the Phoenician workmen who set up these cherubim intended the sphinx-like creatures to be supporters of the divine throne, and it is as such supporters that they are described in Ps 80:2, 1 Sam 4:4, 2 Sam 6:2 and 2 Kgs 19:15.

**1 Kgs 6:37-8.** The use of the old Canaanite names of the months shows that this piece of the account dates from before the Babylonish calendar had become customary among the Israelites.

**1 Kgs 7:2-7.** The house of the forest of Lebanon was intended to be both treasury and armory (cf 1 Kgs 10:17 and Is 22:8), and the hall of the tribunal was built for the public sessions at which the king as chief magistrate heard the grievances of his people. Solomon evidently maintained the tradition of his father and tried some cases himself. He must have been rather more expeditious than David in this business for there is no record of any grumbling at the law's delays such as those which gave Absalom his opportunity to steal the hearts of men. The story of the baby's division may simply be an example of Solomon's quick practical way with such quandaries which ended in an unexpected justice.

**1 Kgs 7:13–22.** The interpretation of the symbolism of the temple and its furnishing is a matter of some uncertainty but what follows here is not I hope illegitimate or unconvincing.

As the worshipper mounted the steps of the temple he saw on either side of the entrance great pillars of bronze, and these were probably surmounted by braziers which were kept continually burning. The smoke that rose from them could be seen from a great part of the town, and at night the flickering flame stood out even more clearly against the dark. To the people of Jerusalem and the surrounding countryside these pillars represented the continual presence of Yahweh in their midst.

In the court south-east of the temple entrance there stood the bronze sea, a great basin borne on the backs of twelve bronze bulls. This was far too huge and high to be of any practical use and seems to have represented Yahweh's power as the circumscriber of the dreadful force of water which the Hebrews feared above all elements.

The pillars and the basin of water were themselves so effective as signs that they influenced the telling of the southern kingdom's view of history and creation. When the men of Judah spoke of the great wonder of Yahweh's protection of his people at the exodus they spoke of two pillars of cloud and of flame which signified his presence as they trudged through the desert, and they spoke of the grand miracle of the crossing of the sea when Yahweh held back the waters. When they wanted to convey their sense of the divine activity at creation they spoke of the two great lights fixed high in the day and night, and of Yahweh's putting an edge to the waters of chaos. The continuity of imagery expressed the continuity of presence and power as Yahweh remained with his people.

The temple furnishings and decorations encouraged the people to think of the building as a microcosm. Yahweh's world was represented by the images of oxen and pomegranates and cedars. And in the midst of this world man in his liturgical action administered the government of animals and plants as the representative of the divine. The temple thus provided an image of the world as man had never seen it, as Yahweh had intended it to be. Those who took part in the ritual possessed a picture of what it must have been like to be alive on the sixth day. The account in Genesis of the first paradise garden is shaped from the temple and its liturgy.

The terms of the creation story are taken from the cult and its rubrics. Everything is described as participating in an ordered ceremonial. The plants and birds and animals perform 'after their kind', like the levites and priests performing their ritual offices 'after their kind' in the sanctuary. The pattern of time in the beginning of the world is not from secular sunrise to sunset but moves after the exemplar of the liturgical day from the eve of the feast, 'It was evening and morning the first day', and the whole world keeps the sabbath rest.

In the centre of this liturgy man is the master of
ceremonies, directing every creature in a cosmic praise.
And he is more than master of ceremonies, for, as
Ezekiel makes obvious from his picture of the first man
wearing the jewelled pectoral, he is the priest of creation.
He is greater even than the high priest of the liturgy.
Though the temple at Jerusalem had no statue of silver
or gold because no dead idol could properly represent the
living God, Yahweh was not without his image. The
declaration 'Let us make man in our image' expresses the
full wonder of man: he is the sign of Yahweh in the
midst of the liturgy. Or at least he is meant to be. The
story of the fall shows why men need a temple. Once the
cosmic liturgy is disrupted there must be some sign of
what the world is to be and what men are to be. The
temple is thus the sign of both the dignity of man and of
his fractured character. To the deuteronomist it seemed
that only while the Israelites held both significances
together were they able to appreciate the temple.

When they regarded the temple as a sign not of the
demand for a reform of their lives before Yahweh but as a
guarantee of their society's permanence whatever their
behaviour they brought another fall upon themselves.
The catastrophe of 586 was thus comprehensible as a
repetition of the exile from paradise. A disobedient
society was not fit to serve in the temple liturgy.

**1 Kgs 8:15–21.** Solomon's address to the people and
their leaders is, like the speech of Moses before the conquest of Palestine (Deut 1:29–31), and that of Joshua at
Shechem (Josh 24:1–25), a deuteronomic recapitulation
of the wonders Yahweh had wrought in the nation's
history. Here the direct object of the speech seems to be
the linking of the davidic family with the Sinai covenant.

1 **Kgs 8:22–54.** The dedication prayer of Solomon expresses the deuteronomist's reinterpretation of the temple after the nation's apostasy and the calamities which resulted from the Israelites' failure to live up to the vocation they had received. No longer is the temple a microcosm bringing together the chosen people before Yahweh that they may receive the divine blessing, it is a house of prayer and repentance (1 Kgs 8:37–40). The symbols have now become pictures of what might have been, not signs of what is.

The older tradition of Jerusalem had stressed the importance of Mount Zion as the dwelling-place of Yahweh, and had suggested that because they were the people of the God of the place they were allowed to encamp about his house. The people's occupation of Palestine had been justified by an appeal to a cultic title-deed.

By the time this passage was composed this kind of justification had been abandoned in favour of an explanation based upon Israel's having conquered the land through a divinely guided campaign. Yahweh led them in the past but does not live among them in the present. The motive behind this change of language was that the deuteronomist was anxious lest the refinements of a transcendental theology got lost in the midst of anthropomorphic talk. The emphasis was now placed upon 'the name' as presence without place. Jerusalem is now thought of as a place where a manifestation of the name took place. There cannot, on this theology, be any confusion between Yahweh's mode of presence and that of the old Canaanite gods in their house-shrines.

1 **Kgs 8:23.** A proclamation which shows how near Israel's religion was to monotheism, and how close was the relation existing between the Israelite and his God as

it was expressed in the covenant and the complementary response of loyal love.

**1 Kgs 8:44–53.** A late passage added in a re-working after the experience of defeat and exile.

**1 Kgs 8:62–66.** This passage reads like an extract from some royal account book. It is likely that the altar which David had used is that old rock now under the dome of the rock. Solomon could not have consecrated the davidic altar afresh, so he must have been consecrating the surrounding areas newly enclosed in the sanctuary.

*1. What is the function of the liturgy in our society? Are there forms of liturgy in our society which are not explicitly religious but which perform a religious function?*

*2. Can liturgy be worked out or must it develop over a period of time?*

*3. Do we require some picture, even if only a picture in our heads, of the divine?*

## 1 Kgs 9:26–10:29. Solomon's successes

This piece of the royal archive material is concerned with various manifestations of Solomon's increasing power. 9:26 ff suggests, with 10:22, that Solomon's men, like the Phoenicians, reached East Africa, and even, it may be, India. The queen of Sheba may have come on a trade mission; recent researches have shewn the dominance of the mercantile Sheban state over its Minaean and Qatabanian neighbours from 900 to 450.

Solomon had other ways of impressing visitors than his sheikh-like aphorisms. The golden ceremonial shields of the temple processions were sufficiently massive and magnificent to rate as the city's ransom in less fortunate days (1 Kgs 14:26), and must have seemed splendid beyond imagination to the tribesmen from Arabia.

The combination of a ready wit, folksy cunning, and a brilliant mercantile flair for making money, gave Solomon a personal prestige which was sufficient for his embarking on monstrous building programmes which would have been opposed if suggested by a man of ordinary grandeur. But such successes as Solomon might claim in foreign affairs and aggrandising projects could not silence every critical voice. Those who resented the corvee and the generally autocratic rule made common cause with those who regretted the passing of the old tribal loyalties and with those good men who saw in the humanism of the court a threat to the purity of Yahwism, until there was a formidable body of opponents waiting only for the opportunity to attack the royal policy in public. Solomon maintained his position undisturbed because he was so successful abroad. The opposition grew more determined through his reign.

The deuteronomist himself gives his sympathies to the opposition. Solomon's marriage to the Egyptian princess, his complacent toleration of Chemosh and Moloch, are seen as the inward causes of the kingdom's political disintegration, and from them the inevitable progression is through the uprisings of Hadan of Edom, Rezan of Damascus, and the first revolt of Jeroboam, to the final division of the davidic empire on the accession of Rehoboam.

## Note

**1 Kgs 11:40.** Because the Pharaoh is named it is for the first time possible in Kings to come near to fixing the precise date of an event in Israel's history by a cross-reference to a foreign calendar. Sheshonk I, founder of the XXII dynasty, ruled in Egypt from 935 to 914.

*1. What authorises a citizen to go outside the constitutionally agreed methods in his opposition to his government?*

*2. Can we now allow an appeal to the divine will as justification for violent opposition to a government?*

# 3
# The divided kingdoms
# 1 Kgs 12:1–16:34

## 1 Kgs 12:25–14:20. Jeroboam 1

The deuteronomist has little interest in foreign affairs,
particularly if they are not conducted from Jerusalem,
and he omits to mention that Jeroboam's first building
and strengthening and military occupations were dic-
tated by the invading marches of Sheshonk, recorded in
the Karnak inscription and the Megiddo stele.

The narrator was more interested in the establishment
of the northern cult at Bethel and Dan. Jeroboam's feast
was evidently a great success in preventing the centralising of the holy in Judah's Jerusalem liturgy.

The southerners attempted in their accounts of the
exodus to show that Yahweh had always hated the
procedures that Jeroboam was adopting in the north (cf
Ex 32:4 and 8), and that Jeroboam was falling into the
sin of idolatry, but there is no reason to accept their
version of Jeroboam's ceremony. The establishment of a
new cult would hardly be done in so imitative a manner of
the traditionally condemned ritual; it is more reasonable
to suppose that the story of the golden calf was inserted
by the southerners into the exodus tale.

Jeroboam obviously aimed at establishing Yahweh's
presence at the northern shrines, he was not trying to

persuade his people to worship new gods. The bulls were evidently thrones of the invisible presence of Yahweh similar to the cherubim of Jerusalem.

A further black-washing of Jeroboam by the historian is to be discerned in the assigning to the northern leader of a great number of shrines for foreign gods, and in the suggestion that he allowed non-levite priests to officiate in his shrines.

**1 Kgs 12:32.** Jeroboam's New Year festival established in the people's minds that he was a king in precisely the same sense that the man at Jerusalem was a king. He was a king at the liturgical centre of Yahweh's cult. At the same time the festival gave the people an opportunity for a celebration of their old covenant in ways derived from the Canaanite agricultural ceremonies.

**1 Kgs 14:19–24.** *Jeroboam's obituary.* This is a typical piece of deuteronomic writing. The notice of the king's death includes a reference to a source of further information and the name of his successor.

The accession note includes the new king's age at accession rather than at the time he became co-regent, the length of his reign, the name of his mother, and a condemnation of his religious policies.

Evidently in both kingdoms the old belief in fertility cults, imitative magic, and ritual prostitution of both sexes as ways of obtaining good crops, constituted a perpetual menace to the Yahwist faithful. The high places, the standing stones, the wooden posts and the dark groves, were associated with the rituals of Hadad and Baal but their pagan and foreign provenance did not make them the less mysteriously fascinating to the Hebrew peasant farmers.

## Three stories set down to show Yahweh's displeasure with the north

*1 Kgs 13:7–32. The man who met a lion.* A folk-tale from prophetic sources of the same easy orthodoxy and immorality as the story of Elisha and the children of Bethel. Miracle stories of this kind show us the lower levels of popular religion.

*1 Kgs 14:1–18. The lady who went to a prophet.* The pathetic hope of Jeroboam's wife for their son, and her search for comfort from the old prophet who had urged Jeroboam's rebellion is turned into a moralistic tale by the deuteronomist who makes from this human unhappiness a grim sign of divine vengeance.

*1 Kgs 15:25 ff.* Even a common assassin is given his place in the divine scheme of sin and doom. Nothing will work for long in the unrighteous state.

**1 Kgs 14:25–15:24.** *An extract from the 'Chronicles of the Kings of Judah'.* This piece of historical writing has been only summarily edited by the deuteronomist. He has added only his conventional obituaries and accession notices, and perhaps subtracted references to the activities of Sheshonk in Israel and the provinces of Judah in order to highlight the spoliation of the temple and the loss of Solomon's golden shields.

**1 Kgs 15:18.** This is the first appearance of the Aramaean kingdom of Damascus as a power in the balance between Judah and Israel. The influence of this state lasted until 732 when the Assyrians over-ran the country.

**1 Kgs 15:22.** Evidently the corvee was still employed by the kings of Judah.

*1. How far should we expect a modern historian to judge past events?*

*2. By what standards, those of the past or of later times, should we allow the historian to judge the events he is recounting?*

## 1 Kgs 15:25–16:34. The northern kingdom of Israel

**1 Kgs 15:25.** This section begins with a revolution to illustrate the unstable character of the northern settlement, and continues with a prophetic fragment in order to show that the instability of the kingdom derives from the continuing anger of Yahweh.

The prophets seem generally to have been conservatives. Jehu, like Ahijah before him and Elijah after, has a simple standard to apply in the making of judgements about the kings—do they encourage the people to see themselves as the people of Yahweh?

**1 Kgs 16:9 ff.** Zimri was a feudal retainer in the military of Elah, who evidently did not have the army with him in his *coup*. Nor, evidently, was the support of the army enough to ensure the immediate success of a candidate since it took five years for Omri to defeat his rival, Tibni. Tibni may have been the candidate of the older, conservative, members of society against the candidate of the young colonels.

**1 Kgs 16:26.** Omri was accounted by the nations as the most significant of all the northern kings after Jeroboam. In the imperial records of Assyria Israel was always referred to as 'the house of Omri'. But the deuteronomist historian is not much interested in such secular glories, and Omri gets the conventionally dismissive obituary notice.

**1 Kgs 16:31.** *Jezebel* is evidently an enemy version of the queen's name. The *Zebul* name coming from *Baal Zebul* has been changed to one referring to zebel, 'dung'. The queen was the daughter of the king of Tyre who at this time dominated the Sidonians.

**1 Kgs 16:32.** Despite the pagan queen Ahab gave his children Yahwist names, and may have been no more involved in the Baal cult of his wife's chaplains than was Solomon in the Egyptian lady's rituals. The Asherah was a symbol of the earth goddess of Canaan.

**1 Kgs 16:33.** Joshua's destruction of Jericho had spawned a tradition of a curse on any who attempted to rebuild the city. The citadel was restored because of a threat of revolt in Moab against Israel's sovereignty. It may be that Hiel was forced to sacrifice his sons for some crime, or perhaps his sons died during the rebuilding and popular superstition associated their deaths with the old curse, or perhaps Hiel obeyed the old ritual of foundation sacrifices and buried his children in the floor of his citadel.

*1. How would we set about testing in our own day whether a man was to be accepted as a prophet?*
*2. Would we want to meet a prophet?*

# 4

# Elijah and Elisha
# 1 Kgs 17:1—2 Kgs 8:29

This huge section of the narrative deals with both the public and private lives of the prophets, and incorporates both genuine historical memories of their words and actions and imaginative legends which grew up about the great men.

The section has been scarcely touched by the deuteronomist. The original account remains to us. And it may be that the Elijah story was finally shaped by Elisha.

## 1 Kgs 17:1–19:21. The Elijah cycle

1 Kgs 17:1–16. *The great famine.* The story of the crows may be read as a folk tale of a hero fed by animals, like the tales of Romulus or Mowgli, or it may be that in the drought a gathering of birds round a feeble beast shewed the prophet where easy meat was to be found. The text could, however, be read without much difficulty as an account of Arab nomads rather than of crows, *arabim* rather than *orebim*. This account of how the prophet was given food would then complement the story of the kindly foreign woman of Sarephath. Aliens would be shewn protecting the prophet from irreligious Hebrews all the way along his journey.

It may, however, seem unreasonable to rationalise the

crows as Arabs in order to put them in line with a story which contains such magical elements as the unceasing supply of meal and oil. Perhaps we ought not to do more than enjoy the folk-tales as celebrations of a hero.

The widow was in the most precarious social position. She was much worse off than the girl who was left a childless widow for no one need marry her to continue the dead man's line. She would have to fend for herself. The story is, therefore, of the humblest in the foreign land doing the will of Yahweh while the Hebrew king works against the divine order.

**1 Kgs 17:18.** The unhappy widow supposes that the presence of the holy man in her house has drawn some hidden sin into the open, rather as a medicament might bring the poison in a body to a headed sore.

Though it is nowhere expressly said that the boy was dead it would be somewhat artificial to introduce so scientific a notion as a coma into the explanation of the tale. The story is not told to assert medical fact but to increase our wonder at the divine work amongst men.

Nor will it do to offer sophisticated explanations relating this event to the primitive practices of other societies. There is no help, for example, in an attempt at paralleling this incident with rituals of contactual magic. In these rituals the sickness is drawn up into some animal or statue placed on the sick man. In the Elijah story it is health which passes from the prophet to the boy. There seems to be no parallel to this feature of the story in any near-eastern source.

A further curiosity in the narrative is its relation to the Elisha story of 2 Kgs 4:34 ff. There is now no telling, though there may be in the future, which came first.

**1 Kgs 18:1–46.** *Carmel.* There are a score of difficulties

about the final shaping of this narrative from earlier
sources but evidently the rain motif gives a unity to the
recital of events which cannot be regarded as manufac-
tured.

It is at least sensible to accept that Elijah was in some
way responsible for a vindication of Yahweh against the
pretensions of a powerful Baal cult in this mountainous
area. Certainly the story gains considerably in point
when it is realised that Hadad, the Baal of the story, was
the Canaanite god of the winter rain and the thunder-
clouds. So the rain and the Yahwistic elements are the
central elements of the event and its telling.

**1 Kgs 18:20.** Elijah makes a bid for the return of the old
covenant life by at once treating the crowd as an assembly of the tribes before Yahweh, rather like those at
Shechem. His use of the twelve stones for the repair of
Yahweh's altar (18:30), has the symbolic meaning of a
bringing together of the tribes for the service of Yahweh,
and this would not be lost either upon those who were on
Carmel or those who heard or read the story later.

**1 Kgs 18:28.** The prophets are not simply working themselves up to a frenzy, they are showing the god what is
needed. In their imitative ritual the god is told to pour
out the life-giving rain on the earth as they pour out their
life blood.

**1 Kgs 18:32.** A similar piece of imitative ritual may lie
beneath the account of Elijah's trench. The ditch is said
to have a capacity of two measures of seed. For the
peasants this may have suggested the ceremony at the
spring sowing time when seed was placed in a trench and
watered to make it sprout quickly. The ritual was
designed to show the rest of the field what was expected
of it.

**1 Kgs 18:36–46.** The prayer to the God of Abraham, Isaac and Jacob is in keeping with Elijah's whole endeavour to recall the old covenant faith to the mind of the people. Their response 'Yahweh is God' is a sign that they got Elijah's message, for it is the old cultic cry of the assembly.

But the threat of Jezebel and her evident power to carry it out show that the Yahwist revival on Carmel was not effective in changing the realities of the political situation. Not until the revolt of Jehu (2 Kgs 9–10), and the murder of Athaliah (2 Kgs 11) was Yahwism in the ascendent in the two kingdoms. Elijah had real cause to despair of ever seeing the restoration of the covenant faith.

The story of the angel and the cake, with its conventional reference to forty days and nights, is evidently part of a formalised folk tale, but the formalisation is purposeful. The divine guide, the food and the mountain are present in the story of Elijah in order that the prophet may be recognised as a new Moses. This is an intention manifest in the account of the cave experience (cf Ex 32:21 ff), and in Elijah's complaint that the covenant is broken by the people.

*1. How does one answer the question 'true or false?' about a fairy tale, a myth or a parable?*

*2. Why have we given up looking for manifestations of divine interpretation in our lives? Do such interventions come now as the Hebrews seem to have supposed they did in their lives?*

## 1 Kgs 20:1–22:54. The interlude of the Syrian wars

In this historical narrative Ahab appears a better man than in the Elijah story. Here he is brave and careful and victorious, and said to be supported by a true prophet against Damascus.

It is probable that the Damascus army's movements were intended to force Ahab into a Levantine alliance against the Assyrians. The whole area was at this time preparing for the confrontation of Qarqar in 853. This accounts for the wish of Benhadad to leave Ahab in charge of Israel while the royal family was removed to Damascus as hostages for the Israel alliance.

**1 Kgs 20:23–34.** The second expedition of Damascus is again shewn to be impotent because Yahweh is with Ahab.

**1 Kgs 20:35–43.** But Ahab has ignored the demands of the holy war and is thus rejected by the orthodox. His death is seen as a punishment for not fulfilling the old demands and for supposing that the prisoners of a holy war belonged not to Yahweh but to the king (cf 1 Sam 15).

The guilt of Ahab's refusal to execute Benhadad is compounded by his resort to murder to wrest Naboth's inheritance from him. The scheme of Jezebel had some subtlety. On the proclamation of a fast of repentance the Hebrews would be ready to accept that sin had been committed and to look for a citizen who had brought disaster on them. The law is observed both in the procedure of witness, elders and popular stoning of the accused, and in the reversion of Naboth's property to the king.

**1 Kgs 22:1–40.** Ahab has married his daughter, Athaliah, to king Jehoshaphat of Judah (2 Kgs 8:18), and is thus the senior partner in quite a strong alliance. Perhaps the Judah king mouths the orthodox part in the discussion of the war-plans because the story derives from a Judah source. Ahab thinks the prophets to be men who influence

God by imitative magic and they respond to this estimate by producing Zedekiah's horns. Jehoshaphat thinks the prophet to be a messenger of Yahweh and his questionings bring out the truth from Micaiah.

It is odd that no one thought of asking Elijah what he thought of the situation. There is a daring and therefore attractive suggestion that *Elijah*, which means 'My God is Yahweh', was the name assumed for his public utterances by this Micaiah the son of Imlah.

**1 Kgs 22:15.** The extraordinarily human thing here is Ahab's pressing for a true answer and not wanting to hear it. He knows what the prophets are up to and yet becomes angry with Micaiah for not playing the same game.

**1 Kgs 22:20.** Yahweh among his princes, like some Canaanite god in his court, is regarded by Micaiah as certainly responsible for the inspiration of the other prophets, but he thinks Yahweh cleverer than the prophets suppose.

**1 Kgs 22:30.** Ahab hoped to bring down the divine doom on Jehoshaphat by dressing him up in his clothes and armour. The device deceives men but not Yahweh. The generals miss Ahab, the archer gets him at a venture. Ahab's obituary is simply the neat deuteronomistic dismissal.

**2 Kgs 1:1–2:20. Folk-tales centring on Elisha**

**2 Kgs 1:2–17.** *Elijah and the mission to Baal Zebub.* This story is evidently of a piece with the later miracle stories of Elisha and comes from similar folk sources. Such stories are commonly generated by such groups as 'the sons of the prophets' to propagate crude wonders about their leader. Here the defeat of both the 'Lord of the Flies' and the king of Samaria must have heartened the conservatives.

**2 Kgs 2:1–9:6.** The fiery story of Elijah's revenges is properly placed not with the old Elijah saga but with the later Elisha miracle stories which have no point but to demonstrate the prophet's power, and to show that the group has a real place in the prophetic work.

**2 Kgs 2:1–18.** This story is designed to substantiate Elisha's claim to be the successor of Elijah and to justify the tradition of the disciples. The story is made up from several pieces—the crossing of the Jordan, which echoes the passage under Joshua and perhaps an early ritual at Gilgal, the inheritance conversation about the double portion of Elijah's spirit which alots the eldest son's portion to Elisha, a memory of some local cult of the fiery horses of the sun (cf 2 Kgs 23:11), and a proud estimate of Elijah's value to the kingdom.

**2 Kgs 2:19–22.** A remembrance of some ritual by which the prophet took away the old curse upon Jericho. The new dish was pure of the contamination of the old influences (cf Jgs 16:11, 1 Sam 6:7, 2 Sam 6:3, 1 Kgs 11:29).

**2 Kgs 2:23.** This foolish tale tells us more about the dervishes and their notions of divinity than it does about Elisha. Elisha seems to have been shaven in a way that proclaimed his prophetic vocation (cf 1 Kgs 20:39).

**2 Kgs 4:38–41.** The common meal may suggest that these dervishes generally eat together and lived perhaps a monastic communal life. The whole story has likenesses with modern moments remedied by adding more salt after exaggerated grumbling about mother's cooking.

**2 Kgs 4:42–4.** The first fruits belonged to Yahweh and we may here have an account of a sacred meal. No comparison is to be made, however, with the accounts of the miraculous multiplication of loaves and fishes in the gospels.

**2 Kgs 6:1–7.** A simple face-saving dervish might well explain the prophet's success when poking around with a stick by the suggestion of miraculous power.

*1. How much is lost when the prophetic insight is organised by sons of the prophets—can religion survive being organised, can it perhaps not survive unless organised?*

*2. Can we, perhaps, not talk of all religions in the same way on this matter, some repudiating and some requiring organisation?*

## 2 Kgs 3:1–9:1. The Elisha cycle

### Elisha alone

**2 Kgs 4:1–7.** There is a temptation to regard this and the following incident as doublets of Elijah stories, but there is no proof of any connection other than of a literary dependence in the manner of telling the story.

The widow is the relict of one of the 'sons of the prophets', and known to Elisha. It would appear that the celibates of the pot story were not the only prophetic group in Israel. And evidently the Carmel group was not exempt from pursuit by such civil obligations as the creditor represents. They must, therefore, have been a more settled prosperous group than the Gilgal dervishes. The story is related with far more Aramaisms than the dervish stories, and evidently comes from a different source.

**2 Kgs 4:8–37.** Elisha is separated from the rest of the household in order that the awful effects of the holy should not come upon them. The distinction between the effects of the magical staff and the prayer of the prophet should be remarked as sign of a sophistication in the narrator.

## Elisha in history

**2 Kgs 3:4–27.** This story reaches its climax in an incident which shows the power of the local cults for both pagan and Hebrew inhabitants. Mesha's sacrifice of his son is aimed at satisfying the anger of Chemosh against Moab and leaving the god free to deal with Israel. Both sides believe that it will work and the Israelites' panic must have confirmed their opinion.

**2 Kgs 5:1 ff.** *Naaman.* The general interchange of faiths between pagan and Israelite is exhibited in this tale of the foreign pilgrim, but at the same time Naaman's disappointment that some ritual was not performed by the prophet shows Israel's growing away from pagan forms.

The pagan muddle is shewn in the expectation of some ceremony like the king's evil, and in Naaman's needing a parcel of earth on which to worship the god whom he has acknowledged as Lord of all.

**2 Kgs 6:8–23 and 6:24–7:20.** Here again the prophet is the true strength of his country, 'the chariots of Israel and the horsemen thereof'. So much reliance was placed on the prophet that at times of defeat it could only be thought that he was not doing his part. There is a fine literary moment when the king reveals the sack-cloth beneath his shirt, and the telling suggests that the narrator of this story belonged to the court and witnessed the incident.

If Elisha at this time kept up his contacts with the dervishes these would have been a ready means for starting a rumour among the Aramaeans, for they would be free to wander between city and camp.

**2 Kgs 8:7-15.** As in the tale of the Shunammite woman, Elisha freely admits that he does not know all the aspects of the event when he is called upon to act. There is no suggestion that the king was murdered though he may have been.

**2 Kgs 9:1-6.** The anointing recognises that the charism of kingship is not necessarily given to the hereditary prince, but only to him whom Yahweh chooses. The popularity of Jehu in the army council marks him out as the man who has the favour of Yahweh, the anointing confirms his charismatic right to the kingdom. Once anointed he is not a rebel but the only legitimate ruler.

*1. Is the holy awful?*

*2. How far is faith-healing to be credited as a divine activity among us?*

# 5
# Decline and fall
# 2 Kgs 9:1—25:30

### 2 Kgs 9:1–10:36. The revolt of Jehu

**2 Kgs 9:1ff.** The dervish lad sent by Elisha to Jehu is both accepted as a messenger of some strange power, and despised as a madman by the young military men. He was probably only attended to by sophisticated men out of a feeling that 'there might be something in it'.

The notice that Joram was wounded may be put in from an older pagan feeling that the king's health was that of the nation, and that a king who lost his vigour should no longer rule. That Joram's palace officers did so little to protect him at the meeting with Jehu suggests that they believed the kingly power to have gone from the wounded man.

Jehu's revolt is set before the reader as a primarily religious action against all the degrading paganisms of the fertility cults and the social evils, like the murder of Naboth, which follow upon these harlotries.

**2 Kgs 9:25.** Jehu's call to Bidqar reveals that he had taken twenty years to rise from driver of a chariot to warden of Ramoth Gilead.

**2 Kgs 9:27.** Ahaziah seems to have been killed by Jehu not primarily because of his command of Judah, though a weakened and disrupted Judah would certainly be unable to interfere in the affairs of a revolutionary Israel, but rather because as brother-in-law of the dead king he might take on the role of avenger in a blood feud.

The king of Judah raced for Megiddo on the plain once he saw that Jehu's horsemen were gaining on his chariot in the hills north of Samaria, hoping that the cavalry regiment remained loyal to Joram.

**2 Kgs 9:31.** Jezebel is certainly not without courage. Her defiant confrontation of Jehu and her scarcely veiled threat that the newest rebel would suffer the fate of Zimri, who was killed a week after his deposing Elah (1 Kgs 16:9–15), show her to fierce advantage. The account of her appearance at the window may be designed to emphasise her foreign ways and serene indifference to Hebrew tradition, since this was the customary place for Egyptian princes to receive men in audience (cf Gen 26:1–14, Jgs 5:28, 2 Sam 6:16, and perhaps Prov 7:6). There is a Samarian ivory tablet in the British Museum illustrating just such a scene as Jezebel at the window.

**2 Kgs 10:1 ff.** The bloody revolution continues with the murders of the male members of the royal house of Omri. 70 is a traditional round number (cf Gen 46:27, Jgs 8:30 and 9:2) and would include not only the children but the brothers and cousins of the late king.

Samaria was a royal city which was the personal possession of the Omride kings and might legitimately have chosen to have a separate ruler from the rest of the country, though the likelihood of such a man standing out against Jehu must have been small.

Politically Jehu was far from a success. He was forced in 841 to submit to Shalmaneser III while Hazael in

Damascus held out against the Assyrians. The only extant representation of a Hebrew king is that of Jehu kneeling for terms before his Assyrian conqueror, which appears on the black obelisk in the British Museum.

Even religiously the deuteronomist is not satisfied that Jehu was quite a success. His line prospers because he destroyed so much of the pagan apparatus in the kingdom but fails at the end because Jehu hesitated to raze the northern shrines of the country gods.

> *1. Do motives really alter actions?*
>
> *2. Are the crimes committed in the name of God properly compared with the crimes committed in the name of liberty?*

## 2 Kgs 11:1–12:21. Athaliah and Joash in the south

From 2 Chron 21 it appears that Jehoram of Judah had had to face conservative criticism of his alliance with Israel, and that he solved his political problems by a series of executions of the leading men and even of some of his own family.

When Ahaziah was killed in his chariot the queen-mother, Athaliah, daughter of Jezebel, seized the opportunity to reign herself and, to effect her ambition, murdered the male remnants of her family. Only the baby prince Joash was rescued by his aunt Jehosheba, daughter of Joram by another mother than Athaliah, and wife of the priest Jehoida.

After six years of hiding in the temple precincts the prince was brought out by Jehoida and a restoration, supported by the priests, the military and the country squires, was effected, Athaliah being put to death with her northern priest. That the historian regarded the whole episode of Athaliah's rule as a usurpation is indi-

cated by the absence of the conventional introduction
and obituary from his account of her life.

**2 Kgs 11:1 ff.** The coronation ritual here must be taken
with that of 1 Kgs 1:33 ff in any reconstruction of the
customary enthronement ceremonies of the kings in
Jerusalem. Here the high priest leads the king to his
special place in the forecourt of the temple, where the
king is invested with the crown and the testimony. The
testimony seems to have been a list of the royal titles (cf
Ps 2:7 and Is 9:6 as well as 2 Sam 7:9 and 1 Kgs 1:47).

**2 Kgs 11:17.** The renewal of the covenant between
Yahweh and the people is based upon the belief that the
king is mediator between divine and human worlds, and
is required at this time because such a royal mediator-
ship has been lacking for the six years of usurpation.

That this Yahwist revolution was accomplished with
only two deaths sets Jehu's revolt in lurid contrast. The
forces of orthodoxy were evidently much stronger in
Judah than in the north even though the country had
been ruled for some years by Jezebel's daughter. But it is
to be noted that while the country people acclaimed the
restoration the men of Jerusalem, who had been dependent upon the queen, were not enthusiastic. It may have
been because of the likelihood of their armed opposition
that Jehoida put the guard round the young prince and
organised the counter-revolution at a time when the
country squires were in the city for a pilgrimage festival.

**2 Kgs 12:7.** Those who are brought up by priests are not
necessarily immune to anti-clericalism, and the clergy,
even those who are acquainted with city financiers, are
not necessarily the best administrators of the funds.

**2 Kgs 12:14.** The ban on frequent renewal of the temple

6—H. 1

vessels was designed to prevent the priests profiting from the sale of those they had too quickly declared derelict.

**2 Kgs 12:21.** Joash's efforts to control the priests brought disaster down upon him (cf 2 Chron 24). He over-reached himself when, in an attempt to quieten discontent at home after losing Gath, he had Jehoida's son Zechariah stoned in the temple precincts. The orthodox rose against him.

*1. How does the significance of a coronation differ from that of an inauguration of a president?*

*2. What are the common roots of so many forms of anti-clericalism?*

*3. What relation should properly obtain between ordination to the service of God and the running of the religious life of the community?*

## 2 Kgs 13:1–17:41. The kingdoms up to the fall of Samaria

**2 Kgs 13.** The kingdom of Israel is here shewn as a vigorous nation blessed by Yahweh with strong kings, victories in war, and sharing in the blessing of the covenant (13:23), and yet. . . . The deuteronomist editor of this piece of northern archive material, which was perhaps brought south by the northern scribes after the fall of Samaria, has added serious notes of caution to the praise of Jehoahaz, who worshipped at Bethel and Dan (13:6), and that of Joash, who did not obey the prophet's command with any eager faith (13:14 ff), and these notes are typical of his editorial policy when treating of any sign of virtue in the north.

**2 Kgs 14:7.** Amaziah has a small victory against Edom

and sends his glove to Joash who has no wish for war but will not put up with a repetition of such irritations. The northern writer makes much of the foolishness of the southern king, and delights in Joash's folk wisdom.

Joash seems to have been mainly concerned with the extension of his economic gains, and having been deprived of his share of the Edomite mercantile spoils (2 Chron 25:6 ff), he aimed at occupying the old Philistine coastal settlements which would have given him command of one end of the Red Sea trade route, and at clearing his southern border of the Judah settlers planted while Israel was being harassed by Hazael. Joash got more than he planned, capturing the king of Judah, ransacking the temple in Jerusalem, and a free run of the border lands.

Amaziah was rather more surprised by this upset. His prestige could not stand such losses because they affected both clerical and military classes. With both Jerusalem and Lachish against him survival was obviously impossible.

**2 Kgs 14:23–29.** *Jeroboam* II. The lack of political interest in Kings is perhaps most apparent in the account of this great king and his work for the establishment of Israel as a power in the Levant. A better idea of the northern kingdom and its prosperity at this time is presented in Amos.

**2 Kgs 14:25.** Evidently the conventional mark of a king's greatness for the historian and his readers is the possession of the lands within the old frontiers of Solomon. It is this unknown Jonah upon whom the tale of the prophet of Nineveh is later fastened.

**2 Kgs 15–16.** The revival of Israel under Jeroboam II was made possible by the distraction of Syria in Assyrian wars from 806 onwards until the success of Tiglath-pileser II made it impossible for Israel to do more than look to its own survival and give up hopes of further conquest.

The assassination of Zachariah of Israel, the last of Jehu's line (15:10), and the following chaos of murder, civil war, and general social unrest (15:14 ff), reveal the weakness of the northern monarchy which could never claim hereditary right to the throne and was always the prey of ambitious colonels and menaced by conservative threats of a renewal of the tribal society. The rebellion of Shallum shows both these forces at work against stable government. Shallum's military revolt succeeds for a month only because the men of Mannasseh will not tolerate an Ephraimite ruler. The Mannasseh attempt to rule with foreign aid quickly gives way to a conspiracy led by the commander of the army.

Pekah was considered by Tiglath-pileser as a hostile king. An Assyrian army marched against the anti-Assyrian league quickly organised by Pekah. Tiglath-pileser III's advance sent Pekah and Rezin of Damascus hurrying to Jotham of Judah with requests for help against the Assyrian. Jotham saw how foolish was their hope of resisting the great power and refused to join in suicide. At this Israel and Damascus turned their armies on Jerusalem and, Jotham dying at the beginning of the war, confronted the new king Ahaz with a show of might on his accession day. The terrified Ahaz rushed for help to the Phoenician god Moloch, and sacrificed his eldest son in the Valley of Hinnom. It was on this occasion that the king was met by Isaiah at the conduit on the Fuller's Field road (Is 7:3 ff), and received the famous prophecy of the birth of the good prince Hezekiah.

Ahaz could not wait for Yahweh's help, he summoned

the Assyrian to rescue him from Israel and Damascus. Tiglath-pileser III came but the cost of rescue was equal to that of defeat.

The Assyrian army swept down the coast in 734 through Israel and Philistia, and established a secure border against Egypt in order to be totally free to deal with the Levantine states. The unfortunate Pekah was assassinated in order that a pro-Assyrian king might be installed by the terrified Israelites, but the men of Damascus were not so quick and in 732 Tiglath-pileser sacked their city, hanged Rezin, and set military governors to rule the country.

Ahaz realised that he had invited the lion into his house and accepted the Assyrian dictates. He was summoned to Damascus to learn the terms upon which he would be allowed to remain in power in Jerusalem. He was forced to bow to the Assyrian gods and to erect an altar to these deities in the very temple of Jerusalem, while the royal door into the temple was bricked up to symbolise the separation of the king from all intimacy with the divine.

**2 Kgs 17:1 ff.** *The last days of Israel.* Shalmaneser V, successor to Tiglath-pileser III, took a close look at the affairs of Hoshea's Israel, and saw that the man was not to be trusted. Hoshea was too friendly with the rival power of Egypt and was summoned to the Assyrian camp where he was arrested. The Israelites, relieved of their Assyrian vassal-king, decided upon resistance, and held out in Samaria for two years behind the defensive walls of Omri and Ahab.

Massive deportations followed upon the Assyrian's final capture of the city under the generalship of Sargon II.

**2 Kgs 17:7ff.** The deuteronomist has a clear notion of why Samaria fell. He lists the offences of the northern kings and their subjects against the liturgical law of Jerusalem: the fertility cults, the making of images, the rejection of the davidic covenant, the golden calves in the hated shrines of Bethel and Dan, the worship of astrological deities, and the sacrifice of children to Moloch, all deriving from the sin of Jeroboam I.

**2 Kgs 17:19.** The deuteronomist, benefiting from the hindsight of 583, can include Judah in the final sections of his condemnation of people and kings.

**2 Kgs 17:24.** The sins of the people are seen by the deuteronomist as fittingly punished in the deportations from the holy land. The Assyrian policy is a sign of chaos come again. The people are in exile and the animals revolt against the folk who have invaded Yahweh's patrimony.

*1. What equivalents are there in our modern western society to the worship of astrological deities and the devourer of children?*

*2. What significance should we attach to the adulation of the prima donna or the pop star?*

## 2 Kgs 18:1–21:26. Judah alone

It might appear that the political history of Judah interested the deuteronomist rather more than that of Israel. The care he takes to record the events of Hezekiah's reign contrasts with his general dismissal of Uzziah and Jeroboam II. But even here the deuteronomist is not really concerned with the political history of the reign except as it illuminates the course of the good king's religious policy.

This primary interest accounts for the extended treatment accorded to the two crises of the end of Hezekiah's reign during the 701 campaign of Sennacherib, for these were affecting the holy city of Jerusalem and the fulfilment of prophecy.

**2 Kgs 18:1 ff.** The record of Hezekiah begins with the conventional deuteronomistic phrases being brought into positive form by the announcement that this king 'did right in the sight of Yahweh'.

It may appear odd that Hezekiah is praised for the removal of the Nehushtan which was thought to have been made by Moses, but the Mosaic attribution is evidently set down by the deuteronomist as a false tradition. The serpent was probably a survival from some ancient fertility cult of the Jerusalem neighbourhood and the story of Num 21:6–9 invented to account for its presence in the temple. Perhaps this sign has something to do with the structure of Gen 3.

**2 Kgs 18:7.** The note of Hezekiah's success in battle is rather a wish-fulfilment than a record of fact. He who reforms the cult must be successful in battle. This is a belief which does not require testing against history.

**2 Kgs 18:17.** The coming of Sennacherib's envoys to Jerusalem is intended as a warning hint of what will happen if Hezekiah relies upon the feeble help that Egypt might offer.

**2 Kgs 18:32.** The Assyrians are full of plain confidence and heartlessly assure the men of Judah that they will be allowed to enjoy their own goods until a time convenient for their deportation.

**2 Kgs 19:2.** Isaiah is the first of the canonical prophets to appear in the histories. His reply to the envoys depends on the supposition that they can know nothing of the ways of Yahweh. The deuteronomist must have appreciated this reference to Yahweh's will, and the assumption that Jerusalem will survive as long as Yahweh is obeyed.

The parallel account of 19:9–20 sets Hezekiah squarely against the Egypt of Taharka.

**2 Kgs 19:21–28.** The curse song, which comes from Isaian circles, not from the great prophet himself, and that of 19:29–31, and the oracles which follow, have the same theme. The success of the foreigner is merely preparatory to a greater triumph of Yahweh among his people.

**2 Kgs 19:35.** Such a plague in Sennacherib's army while it lay near Pelusium is recorded by Herodotus (II, 141).

**2 Kgs 19:36.** The civil commotion of Assyria is shortly described. Esarhaddon himself records a faction war among the followers of various of Sennacherib's sons on the death of the great king. The illness of the king of Judah is, however, given extensive treatment.

**2 Kgs 20:1–19.** *Hezekiah's illness.* This is one of the most shapely of the narratives in Hebrew historical writing. The author has brought together elements of history and folk-tale, political cynicism and psychology, in a story which splendidly affirms the humanity of man and the divinity of God.

The story begins with a typically unpleasant scene of the nineteenth-century novel of realism in which the older Isaiah comes to the young king with the news that he cannot recover. The old shall bury the young. Hezekiah quite naturally turns away and asks the help of a God kinder than the gloating prophet. Yahweh shows that he has a more merciful heart than Isaiah had thought. The prophet is sent back to retract his prophecy of doom and to promise happiness. The prophet's own self-respect is saved by his having a leading part in the medical element in Hezekiah's recovery.

Though the fig has been used for ulcers by Pliny (*Natural History*, XXII, 7), and the doctors of Ras Shamra, it is better to take this element in the story as a manifestation of an innocent delight in such magics as Cinderella's pumpkin or Jack's beanstalk. Lest we dwell too happily on the fairy-tale element the narrator brings himself and us back to the true source of all health and happiness in the next verse. Hezekiah wants a sign from Yahweh. He gets his assurance.

**2 Kgs 20:9.** The king has been lying in his little house on the roof of the palace, a chamber like that of the rich Shunammite woman (2 Kgs 4:10) or that of Eglon, king of Moab, where he sat to receive Ehud (Jgs 3:20). It would be some comfort to the sick man to be cool in the heat of the day. As Isaiah and Hezekiah look down the stair-well Isaiah sees the shadow slowly descending the steps as the sun passes overhead. He says to the king something of this kind: 'Do you think that Yahweh is like a man to change his mind, his will is the same through all history, appearances may make it look as if he is going back on his word but he is not, he like the sun moves ever on and we see his shadow through time and events. Yahweh will remain faithful to his promises to the house of David'. Things, however, went very wrong for Judah, and later generations may well have thought that the shadow had indeed gone back.

Or it may be that Isaiah promised the king that the shadow of death would retreat from him and that there has been a literalisation of images here. Or again, though this is too rationalist a view of signs for me to like, it may be that all this took place on 11 January 689 when there was an eclipse.

**2 Kgs 20:12–19.** After the human tale of Hezekiah and Isaiah, the magic of the figs, and the deuteronomistic interpretation of history, we have an extract from the Jerusalem foreign office minutes. Hezekiah enjoys his illness, he receives the ambassadors of foreign nations, he accepts their good wishes and conducts them himself about the palace showing off his art treasures and his most sophisticated weapons.

Isaiah, no longer friend or physician or prophet but wearing the hat of chief councillor, rebukes him for his thoughtless surrender of classified information about the state of the economy and the stockpiles of armaments. His judgement is that of a sound politician. War and defeat must follow such stupidity.

Hezekiah's reaction is so intensely human that it is difficult to read without tears. Ruin can be faced with equanimity if it is not to come until another generation has to deal with the mess.

**2 Kgs 21:1–7.** Manasseh, perhaps not thinking too well of a father who could accept peace in our time as a policy, appeased the Assyrians by re-installing the altars of Ahab and the cult of the host of heaven.

**2 Kgs 21:8–15.** His actions and those of his son Amon (21:19–22) provide the deuteronomist with the explanation of the destruction of the city which had seemed inviolable before 583.

1. *Can a place or a thing be holy?*
2. *What obligation have we to posterity?*

## 2 Kgs 22:1–23:30. The reform of Josiah and its failure

The deuteronomist is here reaching the origins of his own view of life: the recovery of the primitive version of the book of Deuteronomy and its acceptance by the community as the rule of life for north and south.

Josiah began his reform of the fertility cults in Jerusalem and then worked outwards through Judah from Geba to Beersheba (2 Kgs 23:8) and then finally, while Assyria was engaged with her northern enemies, spreading out into regions recovered from the foreigner. This last stage was stimulated by the rediscovery of the book of the law. The deuteronomist seems to have telescoped these stages into one great movement of popular conversion.

The book of the law itself was probably a scroll of skin like those of Qumran, though it may have been made of papyrus leaves.

The careful management of the reform is evidenced in the recourse to the wife of a minor temple official for a favourable prophecy when Jeremiah and Zephaniah were both active (22:14). Such individual spirits might not have said quite exactly what was required. They might, for example, have not said anything so comforting to Josiah as a promise of a peaceful death, for they might have understood the dangers of the times and warned him of the violence which was about to spring upon the state.

That the deuteronomist thought that the reform should lead to a return to the covenant way of life is evident from the references to the assembly of the people and the covenant renewal at this time, just as if Josiah were beginning a new reign. The king stands at the place of the coronation ritual mentioned in the *coup* of Jehoida (2 Kgs 11:14).

That the reform was managed by some show of force seems likely, for the provinces would not be pleased at the removal of the old shrines, but the opening stage of the Jerusalem reform would have been swift and easy since the royal and ecclesiastical authorities cooperated in the dumping of the fertility cult apparatus into the ravine of the Kidron valley which was beside the temple hill.

**2 Kgs 23:16.** This speedy completeness is seen by the deuteronomist to be a proper fulfilment of the prophecy of 1 Kgs 13.

**2 Kgs 23:20.** This account of Josiah being a bloody reformer in the north is a late elaboration added at a time when such a tale would not have harmed the king's reputation.

**2 Kgs 23:21.** The passover, *pesah*, comes not from the vocabulary of 'passing over', or as is sometimes suggested, from that of 'striking', but from the customary nomadic ritual before a seasonal journey, but it quickly was associated in Hebrew minds with the particular exodus journey, though there is not yet a connection with the feast of unleavened bread.

The novelty of Josiah's passover celebration lies precisely in its transition from a family feast at the local shrine to a pilgrimage festival of the central temple.

**2 Kgs 23:26–7.** While the festival was being celebrated and the reform pursued the sin of Manasseh lurked as a source of doom for the king and his people. The next we hear is that the good king is killed at Megiddo, and those who celebrated the exodus are defeated by the Pharaoh.

Chaos comes upon the people and they foolishly choose Jehoahaz as their king. This poor young man did not survive long enough to be enthroned at the new year festival (cf Jer 22:10 ff). The deuteronomist shows how every king after this is caught in the sin of Manasseh (eg 24:3), and every king himself compounds the royal guilt (23:37, 24:9, 24:19), until the final horror of punishment when Zedekiah's last sight is that of his dead sons (25:7), the walls of the city are broken (25:10) and the people deported (25:21).

The signs of Yahweh's presence and power (25:13) are taken away from the people as the pillars and the bronze sea are cast down. King, country and temple are seen to be at an end.

*1. Should the state establish a religion in a position of privilege?*

*2. Can a reformation of civic and religious life be envisaged that would start now from a restitution of the past order?*

*3. Is it now credible that the clergy should be the leaders of this or any other reformation?*

# Ruth

*Laurence Bright*

# Introduction

Ruth has been the object of a good deal of romantic gush down the ages, the main effect of which has been to obscure its original meaning and purpose. But leaving all that aside, the experts are far from being agreed on what the meaning and purpose is. The one thing that seems fairly clear is that Ruth is a short story, a piece of fiction. There are plenty of examples of the story-form in the old testament; the story of Joseph, for instance, and, more to our point, the story of Tamar in Gen 38. Ruth is modelled on that story, which is about a widow's trick (she dresses as a sacred prostitute) to win her legal rights and an heir. The heir, Perez, is specifically referred to in Ruth 4:12, which is an important clue to the meaning of the later tale as a refinement of the earlier one.

'Later' is pretty certain. Though there have been people to argue for a date as early as the Yahwist author himself (there are people who will argue anything) the general agreement is for a latish date, after the return from exile. Ruth 4:7 is a note on the meaning of earlier Israelite custom, which suggest that it no longer exists and requires explanation. Still, the author is artist enough to avoid anachronisms, and keep up his fiction consistently enough about events some eight centuries before. Ruth is probably a fifth-fourth century work which may well (if it's any comfort) contain earlier traditions.

But why was it written? What, in its author's view, was the main point of the story? This turns to some extent on the question of whether or not the final section, the genealogy of King David, is a later addition or not.

If it is not, but forms the climax of the story, then the descent of the king from a foreign (Moabite) woman is important. It gives some colour to the view that the book is 'really' an attack on the policy of Ezra and Nehemiah, after the return from exile, in forbidding mixed marriages among Israelites—an anti-racist tract. But the book doesn't read that way, and the genealogy probably was added later, as we shall see.

So we should take the story at its face-value. A foreign girl trusts in the power of Israel's God to vindicate her rights under Israelite law. She succeeds in obtaining her inheritance, together with an heir, through the generosity of a God-fearing Israelite. Perhaps the historical context to which we should relate it is that of returning exiles (many of whom would have been of mixed race) finding those in possession at home less sympathetic than they might have expected. The story shows up the selfishness of the possessors through the good qualities of Ruth and Boaz. Anyway whatever the answer, we can still enjoy the tale.

*1. Does it matter that a book of scripture is pure fiction? Or should we try to maintain that it is at least based on earlier material that is historically accurate?*

*2. Read the story quickly through before struggling with the commentary. What does its main point (or points) seem to you to be?*

# 1

# The plight of Naomi and Ruth
# Ruth 1:1-22

### Ruth 1:1–5

The story is set in the time of the judges, roughly from the thirteenth to the eleventh century. The names of the principal characters (apart from Boaz) are introduced at once: our storyteller has a direct style. *Mahlon* means 'to be weak', *Chilion* 'to be pining away' which is an immediate indication that this is fiction. We realise at once that these two are coming to a Bad End. The other names are unknown elsewhere in scripture, and for some of them a meaning can only be guessed. *Naomi* means 'my favourite', *Elimelech* '*melek* (king; cf *baal*, lord) is god'. *Ruth* and the others baffle the commentators, which takes some doing. Names of course mean a lot in Israelite literature, so this again may indicate that the author is some way from his sources.

So a famine is arranged, and our travellers set off for Moab. Probably the peoples on either side of the border were fairly similar, as in the Marches of England and Wales, and the adventure only slightly more hazardous than a journey across those can be. The children married, but within ten years all the men in the family were dead. This really was hazardous. A widow without children, too old to remarry, could rely only on charity. It was essential to return at once and get it.

171

## Ruth 1:6–22

God had 'visited' his people. The word, borrowed from military usage, came to mean God's action to change a situation after he had taken full account of it—often with reference to his final judgement on the Day of Yahweh. Judah was once more a place to live in, but it seemed mad to bring the two young Moabite widows back to a land where they were less likely to find husbands, their one real hope of survival. Yet in Naomi's somewhat rhetorical remark about the impossibility of her setting things right by having further sons, who on growing up would be required by Israelite law (Deut 25:5–10) to marry their brother's widow and so continue his name, the author already hints at the central theme of his story. Perhaps not a brother, but some other kinsman will come to the rescue in this way? But the hope is too tenuous for Orpah, who goes home.

Ruth, by contrast, has faith in the future. In her famous reply (1:16–17) she forsakes her home, her people and her gods in order to take on those of Naomi who, humanly speaking, can offer her nothing. The implication is that God can help those who trust him even when things look hopeless.

Naomi renames herself 'Bitter' as more suitable to her situation. Her misfortunes are the work of Yahweh, a common Hebrew idea before devils were discovered. The real meaning of *Shaddai*, translated 'Almighty' in RSV, is unknown; it is mostly used in late writings, but could well be a primitive name for a god later identified with Yahweh.

They return at the beginning of the barley harvest (passover) and the scene is set for the central episodes of the story.

*1. Had Ruth been an Israelite, Naomi a Moabite, and the god chosen by Ruth Chemosh, we would have called it apostasy rather than faith on her part. Comment, and perhaps look for modern parallels.*

*2. Is there any real reason (apart from the prejudice of theologians) against saying God is the cause of evil in the world?*

# 2

# Boaz and Ruth
# Ruth 2:1-3:18

### Ruth 2:1–7

Naomi and Ruth must by now have been close to
starvation, if they depended on what the girl could pick
up by gleaning. The law stated 'when you reap the
harvest of your land, you shall not reap your field to its
very border, nor shall you gather the gleanings after
your harvest, you shall leave them for the poor and the
stranger. I am the Lord your God' (Lev 23:22; cf Lev
19:9, Deut 24:19). Perhaps we could hardly expect
ancient Israel to go beyond this form of charity, by
trying to ensure there were no poor, or that strangers
could actually earn a living. Ruth happens to reach the
field belonging to their rich relation, who as yet knows
nothing about her. We are meant to understand that God
is directing her steps.

Boaz is introduced as a God-fearing man: his greeting
to his workers has come down into modern liturgy. He
takes an immediate interest in Ruth, but cautiously first
enquires about her family.

### Ruth 2:8–23

The story now begins to quicken its pace. Boaz shows his
appreciation of Ruth's loyalty to Naomi, of which he has
now been told, by offering her his protection. She is to

stay in his fields and share in the refreshments. Once again the author reminds us that this is God's doing. Ruth has come under the protection of Yahweh, of whom Boaz is only the instrument (2:12–13).

There is something slightly ridiculous to a modern eye in the picture of Boaz's workers deliberately dropping corn for Ruth to pick up. Why not just give her some? But such a direct interest on the part of the master would at once have damaged her reputation.

Anyway she manages to have picked up an ephah of barley by the evening. The authorities seem to vary on the size of the ephah, but average it out at a bushel, which isn't a lot of help to us confirmed urban dwellers. Still it seems a great deal of barley to have got in a day's gleaning, and as she kept this up (2:23) for some two or three months, one wonders what they were doing with it all. But this is, after all, only a story, and perhaps we should no more question the details than ask after Lady Macbeth's children. Naomi learns from Ruth that Boaz is the source of this windfall and reveals that he is a near kinsman. Once more the reader's interest is quickened, aware as he would have been that a legal obligation was being touched on. To us it seems odd, again, that if Naomi knew about this all along she shouldn't have gone about matters more directly, but even in Israel the poor, and women in particular, were pretty helpless. The way things are working out is again attributed (2:20) to the steadfastness of Yahweh, who never forsakes those who trust in him.

*1. Can we today still see the hand of God in everyday events?*
*2. Is there any justification for thinking that we should manage to keep our heroine off the streets more efficiently? read Orwell's* Clergyman's Daughter).

## Ruth 3:1-18

After Naomi's delicacy and hesitation over the previous months, her sudden determination to catch a son-in-law comes as something of a surprise. We are given no hint of any development in the relationship between Boaz and Ruth; we are in a very different world from that of Miss Austen. The justification for Naomi's plot again turns on the duties of a kinsman (3:2). Dressed to kill, Ruth is to go to where Boaz is asleep at his threshing-floor (he cannot risk his corn being stolen) and lie down beside him. The phrase (3:4) 'uncover his feet' is the usual Hebrew euphemism for his genitals. Fairly clearly nothing happened, since if the pair had slept together the point of 3:12 (the nearer kinsman) would have been lost. Presumably, then, the sexual reference is to increase the reader's curiosity as to what the outcome might be. It continues in the next verses, for 3:8 'he turned over' implies that Ruth was lying beside him (not at his literal feet) as does the spreading of the skirt in 3:9 (try doing this to someone at your feet).

Still the point is in 3:9. Ruth asks Boaz to marry her, by the protective gesture with the skirt (cf Deut 22:30). But the reason why she has the right to do this is that he is the 'kinsman'. The word in Hebrew (Naomi has already used it in 2:20) is *goel*, meaning 'protector' in several senses. Thus in Num 35:19 he is the 'avenger of blood' who puts the murderer of his relative to death. In Lev 23:25 he has to redeem landed property when this has been alienated. He is always the closest relative. Deut 25:5-10, which we shall have to look at in chapter 4, speaks of the obligation of the *Yabam*, or brother-in-law, to marry a childless (ie without a *son*) widow and so perpetuate his brother's name. The word *goel* does not seem to have been applied to him before the book of Ruth, but it was a natural extension: family ties were taken pretty seriously in Israel. Finally it should be mentioned that God is frequently referred to as the *goel* (redeemer) of Israel in the second Isaiah (eg Is 41:14, 43:1, 43:14, etc) and in the psalms (eg Ps 19:14). There must certainly have been overtones of this in a late work like Ruth, so full of the workings of providence.

Boaz's reply (3:10) seems odd at first sight: but this is not a romantic love-tale. He has taken the point that Ruth in asking him to marry her is continuing her loyalty to Naomi and Elimelech (and their God who has adopted her) by perpetuating Elimelech's name through his *goel*. She might well have attracted a younger man.

The suspense is allowed to continue; we now learn that there is a closer relative, who has the first option on playing *goel*. Boaz promises to clear things up in the morning, and sends her home as soon as it is safe, though before anyone could recognise her. She gets some more barley (what the amount was this time we fortunately don't know) and returns to Naomi, who realises that the plan has succeeded.

*1. What has this chapter to say about the position of women in Israel?*

*2. Would it be helpful to adapt the* goel *institution to the modern world?*

*3. In the new testament Christ is also called the* goel *(redeemer) of Israel. How does the book of Ruth help to correct the false idea of redemption we are so often given?*

# 3
# Boaz the redeemer
# Ruth 4:1-17

Boaz goes to the gate of the town, where business was done, and waits for the nearer kinsman to pass through on his way to the fields. He also collects judges, since this is to be a legal process (cf Deut 25 : 7). He first speaks of the traditional right of the *goel*, to redeem Naomi and Elimelech's land. The man is willing to do this. But Boaz adds that this involves marriage with Ruth, in order to continue Elimelech's line. This further function of the *goel* must have been customary by the time the book was written; an innovation would have needed more explanation. The law (Deut 25:5) only required brothers of the dead man to do this, not more remote kinsmen. But this is too much for the kinsman, since it would mean that the land he had bought would go to his children by Ruth. The reader sighs with relief. Boaz knew what he was up to.

The author feels he has to explain the piece of symbolism which follows—the kinsman gives his sandal to Boaz in order to ratify the deal. As Ps 60:8 shows, putting your shoe on land, or casting it over, was to claim possession. But here there are obvious overtones of the different custom in Deut 25:9, where the woman whom a *goel* has refused to redeem pulls off his sandal and spits in his face as well. This seems to be the only use of the rite of pulling off a sandal in earlier times, so the talk of earlier custom is puzzling unless, as is certainly possible, the author knows of such not recorded elsewhere in scripture. Or maybe this is just a modern worry.

Nothing remains but to round matters off, Boaz declares that he has bought both Elimelech's land and his daughter-in-law (first things first): Elimelech's name will now continue in his descendants (this being the only form of immortality recognised until quite late in the old testament). The deal is ratified by the witnesses, with a blessing on Ruth, comparing her with the traditional ancestress of Israel. Rachel in particular was connected with Bethlehem, through her tomb (Gen 35:10) and the blessing might well be the one commonly used in Bethlehem.

The reference to Perez (4:12) recalls the story of Judah and Tamar (Gen 38) on which the book of Ruth is modelled. Moreover, according to the genealogy in 1 Chron 2:5 and 2:9–11, Perez was an ancestor of Boaz, and by another line (2:19) of Ephrath, associated with Bethlehem—the names in these stylised genealogies are as much clans and places as people. We are evidently dealing with a Bethlehem tradition. It is a little surprising that the children in 4:12 are attributed to Boaz rather than Elimelech, since the story turns on this, but the two are, after all, clan members and so share them in Israelite eyes—Naomi, as legal mother, gets similar treatment in 4:4–5, after the birth of the child.

The prototype story of Gen 38 ends with the naming of the child, and as is common in Hebrew, the names relate to the story. Gen 35:18 is another instance. But here there is no parallel. Instead of being named so as to sum up and complete the story (eg as 'Son of Elimelech' or 'of Naomi') the child is simply called Obed ('servant').

This has led commentators to suppose that Obed has been introduced here from the genealogy in 1 Chron 2:11, replacing an original name. The story is patently not one about the ancestry of David. But of this more in a moment.

*1. Do you agree that the story is complete as a study in family loyalty and keeping up of ancient Israelite traditions, suited to the post-exilic period?*

*2. What parallels can you think of in other (ancient or modern) literature?*

# 4

# Appendix
# Ruth 4:18-22

Whatever may be said of 4:17, this genealogy is fairly clearly from a later hand. Introduced by the Priestly formula, 'these are the descendants', it seems to be derived from 1 Chron 2, though there are various discrepancies with other chapters of 1 Chronicles which need not concern us—these are tribal genealogies, not literal ones. But Elimelech is completely ignored, so that the main point of the book is lost.

A different point replaces it. Boaz, and thus Ruth, is presented as the ancestor of David. The presence of a foreigner in the line of the hero-king is no doubt meant to recall to Israel, at a time when exclusiveness had become the order of the day (cf Ezra 10) that God's providence works in unexpected ways. This is the sense in which Matthew incorporates the genealogy into the beginning of his gospel, underlining the point by introducing Rahab the harlot from Jericho (Josh 2:1) as the mother of Boaz. Rahab, who like Ruth, has chosen Yahweh against all appearances, had become a christian heroine (Heb 11–31). Though yet more edifying this takes us further still from the tale of Ruth of Moab.

*1. Is the Hebrew convention of manipulating genealogies any better or worse than our taste for accuracy in them?*

2. *Do you think that the point of the main tale and of the added genealogy are in fact reasonably in accord? Or does the addition mess up the story?*